Introduction

The early Irish had an extraordinary variety of personal names. Indeed, some twelve thousand names are recorded in the early sources. Yet only a handful of names drawn from a rich heritage are in current use in Ireland. Thousands of them fell out of fashion at a very early period. In the later middle ages the range of names in general use was greatly narrowed and when English became the dominant language of the country, common English, biblical and classical names frequently replaced native ones. This book contains just under a thousand Irish names selected from the annals, genealogies, mythology and historical literature of early medieval Ireland. We have also admitted a number of borrowed names which were once (or still are) well established here, some introduced by early Irish clerics, some by the Anglo-Normans. Any selection poses problems of choice and we have attempted to follow some principles. For instance, we have tried to include all the most popular native names in use in Gaelic Ireland down to the nineteenth century together with their variant forms and their sometimes odd translations into English. We have also included rarer and more obscure names for different reasons: because they were (or are) traditionally attached to particular families, because they are the names of once famous saints, kings or heroes, because many of them are euphonious and may appeal to people for their sound or sense.

Irish names are enjoying an increasing popularity and we have tried to encourage that fashion because we believe that names carry cultural values and have powerful historical associations. Above all we have tried to extend the range of Irish names currently available by drawing on the rich record of the past, much of which remains unpublished or hidden from the general public in scarce or expensive scholarly books. We have also tried to deepen appreciation of Irish names by giving their historical and family associations, the surnames which derive from them, the famous people in mythology and history who bore them and, where possible, their meaning. We have noted which names were borne by Irish saints and the associations and feast-days of these saints.

Because of the sheer abundance of Irish names, borrowed ones have only been sparingly admitted. Recent borrowings, exotic variants and fancy-names have been almost totally excluded in favour of those which have been established here for centuries. Even then, we have had to be highly selective. For example, the vast bulk of the new names brought into this country first by the Normans, and later by the English, belong to the common fund of western European names. Many of these have been omitted because they can be found in any good dictionary of names. However, a large number of those which took firm root here, developed Irish forms or have interesting associations are included.

In *one* language, with the passage of time, names develop many variant forms and spellings. In Ireland, with the widespread replacement of Irish by English in the nineteenth century and before, change was even more marked. People substituted English names for Irish or made unusual, not to say bizarre, translations which differ from time to time and from place to place. This poses the problem of finding a standard form, a problem which we cannot say we have solved satisfactorily. We have decided to use an alphabetical order and have given first and as head-word the older Irish form, second the modern Irish form or forms, and third the various anglicised forms and translations where they exist. In that way, all the various forms of each name are placed together under one head-word and the index is designed to refer the reader to the appropriate head-word in each case. Examples are given below in the section 'How to use this book'.

Irish names are constructed in a number of different ways. Some contain a single element, others two or more elements

Gaelic Personal Names

DO THIARNÁN
TUGAIT SGRAIBHNE AN LEABHAIR-SEO

Gaelic
Personal
names

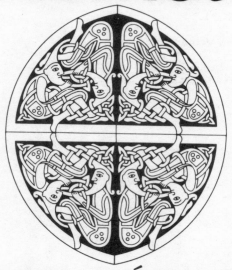

Donnchadh Ó Corráin
Fidelma Maguire

ap

THE ACADEMY PRESS · DUBLIN

First published 1981
Copyright © 1981Donnchadh Ó Corrain and Fidelma Maguire

ISBN 0 906187 39 7

Jacket design by Frank Spiers

Typeset in the Republic of Ireland by M.A. O'Brien
Printed in Great Britain by Blackwell Press

The Academy Press
124 Ranelagh, Dublin 6, Ireland

linked closely to form a compound or just loosely joined together. *Áed*, *Lug*, *Cian* are examples of the first type; *Murchad*, *Donnchad*, *Cú Ulad*, *Máel Muire* examples of the second type. While the ultimate meaning of some names is self-evident, many others are extremely obscure. As Professor M.A. O'Brien has said: 'unlike an ordinary word the meaning of which can be determined, a name has no meaning'. We do not, for example, call a child *John* because it means in Hebrew 'Jehovah has favoured', nor do we associate this meaning with a person so called in everyday life. Likewise, a girl is not called *Rose* because of the meaning of the name—it is derived from Old German *hros* 'a horse'. A name rapidly becomes a label with many more powerful associations than its meaning, which generally fades into the background. The meanings suggested in this book are, in many cases, no more than educated guesses. Many names may have been borrowed from earlier languages completely unknown to us and may simply have been given a Celtic form. Had we no knowledge of Irish and the change from Irish to English in Ireland, who could guess that *Cud* derives from *Conchobar*, *Barney* from *Brian*, *Dolty* from *Dubaltach*, and *Nappy* from *Finnguala*? Yet a scholar dependent on English alone could suggest obvious, highly uncomplimentary, and, as we know, totally wrong meanings for these names. Nonetheless, the original meaning of some names appears to be clear enough.

A large class of names is derived from colours: *bán* 'white' (Báine, Bánán); *ciar* 'black, dark' (Ciar, Ciarán, Ciarnat, Ciarmac, Ciardae), *corcc* 'red, crimson' (Corcc, Corccán); *crón* 'saffron-coloured, yellow, swarthy' (Crónán, Crónéne, Cróinsech); *donn* 'dun, light-brown' (Donn, Donnchad, Donngal); *dub* 'black' (Dubán, Dubacán, Donndubán, Súldubán); *finn* 'bright, white' (Finn, Finnsech, Finnétan, Finnguala); *flann* 'blood-red' (Flann, Flannacán, Flannán, Flannat); *glas* 'green to greyish blue' (Glass, Glaisne, Glassán); *gorm* 'dark, swarthy, black' (Gormán, Gormlaith); *lachtna* 'milk-coloured' (Lachtna, Lachtnán); *ruad* 'red-haired' (Ruadán, Ruadacán, Ruaidrí); *temen* 'dark' (Temnén). In early Ireland there were social nuances attached to colours. Dubhaltach Mac Firbhisigh, the seventeenth-century antiquary

3

and genealogist writes: 'Everyone who is fair-skinned, brown-haired, bold, honourable and daring . . . is of the true Gaeil. Everyone who is fair-haired, honourable, tall and musical . . . is of the Tuatha Dé Danann (the god-folk). Everyone who is black-haired, vociferous, ill-doing, tale-telling, vulgar, stingy and mean . . . is of the Fir Bolg (here meaning the original pre-Gaelic inhabitants of Ireland)'. In Irish literature generally the bright colours are considered to be noble, aristocratic and indeed beautiful, for brightness of skin and hair is very much part of the ancient Irish ideal of beauty in men and women. We do not know if these notions had any effect on name-giving.

Another very large class of names is formed from the names of animals and living things. *Cú* 'wolf, hound' is one of the most frequent elements in names. The hound was the symbol of bravery and nobility in early Ireland and is very clearly distinguished from the *mata* 'dog, cur', a term of abuse and derision if applied to a person. The element *cú (con)* is present in hundreds of Irish names: Conall 'strong as a wolf or hound', Conamail 'wolf-like', Conchobar 'wolf-lover', Conmacc, Macc Con 'son of the wolf', Cú Mara 'sea-hound', Cú Ulad 'hound of the Ulstermen', Cúán, Conán 'hound'. In Ireland, the wolf was a tabu animal and terms other than his name were used to describe him e.g. *fáelchú* 'howling hound', *fáelán* 'the howler', *cú allaid* 'the wild hound' and *mac tíre* 'son of the land'. These in turn became personal names. The bear was also a tabu animal in Ireland as in other European countries and the names for the bear *art* and *mathgamain* gave rise to such personal names as Art, Artán, Artucán, Mathgamain, Mathgen. Other animal names in use were: *banb* 'sucking pig' (Banbán, Banbnát), *bran* 'raven' (Bran, Branán), *brocc* 'badger' (Broccán, Broicsech), *crimthann* 'a fox' (Crimthann, Crimthannán), *cuilén* 'whelp' (Cuilén), *dam* 'deer' (Damán, Damnat, Damairne), *elit* 'hind' (Eiltíne), *ech* 'steed' (Eochu, Eochaid, Echen, Echmarcach), *fiad* 'deer' (Fiadnat), *fuinche* 'scald-crow', here equated to the war-goddess (Fuinche), *géis* 'swan' (Gelgéis), *magor* 'salmon' (Magor), *mucc* 'pig' (Muiccíne), *odor* 'otter' (Mac Uidir, Odrán), *rón* 'seal' (Rónán, Rónnat); *os* 'deer' (Oissíne, Osnat), *ség* 'hawk' (Ségéne, Ségnat); *sord* 'ram' (Sord).

4

Other names derive from what must have originally been nicknames describing more general personal characteristics: *Ágdae* 'contentious', *Aicher*, 'swift, sharp', *Báeth* 'vain, foolish', *Becc* 'little', *Béoán* 'lively lad', *Cáem* 'beloved, beautiful', *Cass* 'curly-haired', *Cennétig* 'ugly head, rough head', *Cennselach* 'overbearing', *Dímmusach* 'proud', *Dian* 'swift', *Duaibsech* 'melancholy', *Fachtna* 'malicious', *Lonngargán* 'fierce and eager person'—to name but a few that come to mind. On occasion, these are combined with other elements to make compound names: e.g. *Báethgalach, Beoaéd, Finncháem, Beccenech, Diangalach, Cassán* and others.

Still other names derive from words describing various offices, functions and social positions. Amongst these we may cite *flaith* 'a lord' (Flaithem, Flaithbertach, Flaithrí), *tigern* 'lord, warlord' (Tigernán, Tigernach, Fortchern, Cathchern, Lugthigern, *rí* 'king' (Rígán, Rian, Laechrí), *bard* 'poet' (Barddán, Rígbarddán), *cléirech* 'cleric' (Cléirech, Cléirchíne), *manach* 'monk' (Manchán, Mainchíne), *goba* 'smith' (Goba, Gobbán, Goibniu, Gobnat). Some reflect riches in lands or goods (Sétach, Selbach, Cétach, Tírech, Toicthech) whilst others, indeed, indicated that their original bearers held no high social rank. Some names derive from the names of dynasties or family-groups: Connachtach, Cú Chonnacht from *Connachta*, the descendants of Conn who gave their name to the province of Connaught; Ultán from *Ulaid*, the ancient dynasty which gave its name to the province of Ulster, *Laígsech* from Lóigis, the dynasty which gave its name to the district of Laois. True locatives, names derived from place-names, are very rare in Irish except in the form of loose compounds, e.g. *Cú* 'hound' by metaphor 'outstanding warrior' + place-name, or *Dub* 'dark man' + placename. Cú Bladma 'hound of Slieve Bloom', Cú Faifne 'hound of Faffand' (an area in ancient Offaly), Dub Emna 'dark man of Emain Macha' may serve as examples.

The Irish, as most peoples, distinguish sharply between male and female names. I have, however, noticed that the following are common to both sexes: Ailbe, Áine, Barrifind, Cellach, Columb, Feidlimid, Finn, Flann, Macha, Móen, Medb,

5

Mongfind, Séigíne. More surprisingly, there are examples of the (normally) male names Gormmán, Máel Bracha, Máel Étig, Máel Meda, and Máel Muire being applied to women. With few exceptions, all names ending in -án, -éne and -íne are masculine. These may be frequently turned into female names by substituting -nat or -sech e.g. Aedán: Aednat, Beccán: Beccnat, Biccíne: Biccsech, Breccán: Breccnat, Cáemán: Cáemnat, Ciarán: Ciarnat, Crónán: Cróinsech, Crommán: Cruimmsech, Donnán: Duinnsech, Damán: Damnat, Dúnán: Dúnsech, Gobbán: Gobnat, Lugán: Luigsech, Oissíne, Ossnat. Quite a number of female names are compounds containing the (element) word *flaith* as a second element, e.g. Coblaith, Tailefhlaith, Túathfhlaith and many others. The word *flaith* means both 'sovereignty' and 'sovereign, prince' in Irish. It must have originally meant 'queen, princess' in female names but at an early period it seems to have come to be regarded as an ending for feminine names. Compare the pairs Dúnfhlaith: Dúnán, Gormlaith: Gormmán, Sáerlaith: Sáerán, Túathfhlaith: Túathán, (Túathal, Túathgal). Similarly, the word *tigern* 'lord', always masculine in the literature, occurs in feminine names where it must mean lady e.g. Cáeltigern, Caíntigern.

Since Irish society was a patriarchal society and since most of our historical records concern themselves with the activities of men rather than women, far fewer women's names are preserved and this will be evident to the reader of this book. Fashions in names varied from age to age and apparently from sex to sex. Certainly, women seem to have been far readier to borrow foreign names. In the later middle ages *Mór* is by far the most popular female name, followed closely by *Sadb* and *Gormlaith*; *Finnguala* appears next, followed by the borrowed name *Sibán*; *Derbforgaill*, *Ben Mide*, *Bébinn* and the borrowed names, *Caiterína* (in its various forms) and *Margrég* (Margaret) are next in popular favour. However, very early names e.g. Étaín, Medb, Taillte, Ailbe and others remained in use. If we may judge from earlier sources, *Sadb*, *Cacht*, *Mór*, *Gormlaith* and *Orlaith* were the five most popular names in twelfth-century Ireland.

The development of early Irish names, their etymologies,

6

hypocoristic (pet-name) forms, back-formations, shortened forms and derivatives is a matter of much fascination for the scholar and the historian; their forms and origins conceal much of the history of Ireland within them; and from them derive the vast majority of the surnames in use in Ireland today. Names themselves and the giving of them, if we may judge from early literature and folk-tradition alike, have always been a matter of lively interest both to their bearers and to those who gave them. With the revival of interest in Gaelic Ireland at the beginning of the century and with the Anglo-Irish literary movement, there was naturally a renewed interest in Irish personal names, the majority of which had been swept away in the language change of the nineteenth century. As a result a limited number of the older (and, one may add, rarer) personal names, e.g. Cáemgen (Kevin), Brénainn (Brendan), Iarlaithe (Jarlath) etc. came into use again. However, apart from some remarkable articles in the *Gaelic Journal* [1], some papers in the less accessible Celtic journals, and Patrick Woulfe's *Irish names for children* [2] little has been made available on Irish personal names. It might be added that the subject has not attracted the scholarly attention which it deserves. It is hoped that the present volume may serve as an introduction, however inadequate, to the riches of Irish personal names.

Bishopscourt,   D.Ó.C.
1980   F.M.

1. J.C. Ward, 'Irish personal names I. Co. Donegal', *Gaelic Journal*, ix, no. 104 (Feb. 1899) 319-21; P.T. McGinley, 'Irish personal names II. Co. Antrim', *ibid.*, no. 105 (Mar. 1899) 344-5; S. Ó hAnnabháin, 'Irish personal names. Oirghialla.', *ibid.*, no. 119 (1900) 565-7; A. Ó Ceallaigh, 'Irish Christian names', *ibid.*, xi, no. 135 (Dec. 1901) 197-205.
2. Patrick Woulfe, *Irish names for children* (Dublin: Gill 1923); reprinted 1967, revised edition (by Gerard Slevin) with preface and some additions, 1974. Ronan Coughlan, *Irish christian names* (London and Edinburgh: Johnston and Bacon 1979) is quite unreliable and inaccurate on many points.

How to use this book

Arrangement of Names

The book is arranged in alphabetical order. Generally, in the case of each entry, the name is first given in its early Irish form. This is followed by a colon, after which the modern Irish form is given. If there are a number of forms, this is indicated. This is followed by a guide to the pronunciation of the name, enclosed in round brackets. There is an indication as to whether the name is masculine, feminine or common followed by the meaning or derivation of the name — in so far as it is known. The length of the entry on each name varies with the importance of the name and the amount of information available about it. All names prefixed by an asterisk (*) are borrowed names.

The index should be consulted for names which cannot be found at first glance, for variant forms of names and for anglicisations of Irish names. To take some examples:

Noreen will not be found in alphabetical place under this form because it is not an Irish form or the oldest form. Turn to the index. The reader is directed to *Onóra*, the oldest Irish form, under which all the variant forms are given.

Aonghus will not be found in alphabetical place under this form because it is not the older form of the name. Turn to the index. You are directed to *Oengus*, the earlier form, where the information needed is given.

Your name is *Hannah*. No entry is found under that

name. Turn to the index. You find yourself directed
to three names: *Áine, Onóra, Sibán*. Look them up and
you find that *Hannah* has been used as a form of each
of these names.

Pronunciation
The guide to pronunciation given in parenthesis generally
refers to the modern Irish form. It gives only a very approxi-
mate indication of the correct pronunication(s). For more
exact information, a good speaker of Irish should be consulted. If the earlier form of the name is found attractive, we
see no good reason why the reader should not pronounce it
as he feels fit. The pronunciation of Old Irish is uncertain
anyway and Irish medieval scribes, it may be added, treated
the forms (and pronunciations) of names with great freedom.

In Irish, the stress (which is strong) generally falls on the
first syllable. Vowels in later syllables, unless they are long,
are pronounced very lightly. The following hints will help
the reader in using the pronunciation guides.

(a) is roughly equivalent to English *law*
(e) is roughly equivalent to English *veil*
(ī) is roughly equivalent to English *fee*
(ō) is roughly equivalent to English *show*
(ū) is roughly equivalent to English *rood*
(ei) is roughly equivalent to English *vine*
(ow) is roughly equivalent to English *owl*
(ch) is roughly equivalent to Scottish *loch*

In Irish, short vowels are simply shortened forms of the long
vowels. In this pronunciation guide short u (u) is rendered as
unstressed a (a).

Irish consonants have two qualities: palatal and non-palatal
(velar). Palatalisation is produced by raising the front of the
tongue towards the hard palate. All palatalised consonants
are indicated by the symbol ', e.g. Crónsech (which has
palatal (n) and (s) is represented as krōn'-s'ach.

Conventions of Spelling
The following conventions are followed. The form *mac Néill*

usually refers to the standard Irish for 'son of Niall', whereas *Mac Néill* refers to the Irish form of the surname of which *MacNeill, McNeill* are anglicisations. The uses of ua/Ua and ó/Ó are analagous. In classical Irish *mac* followed by a vowel becomes *mag* or *meg*. The standard middle Irish plural of *mac* is *meic*. From the 9th century onwards, surnames began to be formed by prefixing *mac* or *ua/ó* (grandson) to the father's or grandparent's name. (*Uí* is the plural of *Ua*).

a

*AARON m. The name of the brother of Moses and high-priest of Israel. It was borrowed from the Bible and used sparingly by early Irish churchmen. St Aaron, a British martyr, was put to death at Newport in south Wales in the reign of Diocletian. The name is very rare in continental sources.

*ABAIGEAL f. In the Bible Abigail is the name of the wife of Nabal and, after his death, of King David. It was very common in Ireland in the nineteenth century especially in the form *Abaigh* (abī). In the south it was used as a genteel 'translation' of the native name *Gobnat* (which see).

ÁBARTACH: ÁBHARTACH (āv-art-ach) m. This name was in use among the Uí Iffernáin (Heffernans) of Dál Cais amongst others. In the Finn-tales Ábartach is the father of the beloved of the warrior Cáel. The name gives the modern surname O Haverty.

ABBÁETH: ABAOTH (a-bē) m. Meaning perhaps, 'lustful'. A rare name in use among the early Leinstermen.

ABBÁN: ABÁN (ab-ān) m, 'little abbot'. The name of a Leinster-born hermit saint of the late sixth or early seventh century. According to tradition, he baptised St Finnian of Clonard. His feast-day is 27 October.

*ABÉL m. The name of the biblical Abel which was borrowed by early Irish clerics such as the monks Abél of Emlagh in Meath (†747), Abél of Portumna (†754) and the scribe Abél who was slain by Viking raiders in 922.

11

ABLACH: ABHLACH (av-lach) f.   Perhaps meaning 'having apple-trees, like an apple-tree'. The best-known bearer of the name was an Ulster princess and mother of Eochaid mac Fiachnai, King of Ulaid (†810).

*ABNER m.   The name of the biblical Abner, cousin of Saul and commander of his army. It was borrowed by such early Irish clerics as Abner, abbot of Emly (†760) and Abner, abbot of Killeigh (†827), but it never became popular.

ACHALL (achal) f.   A mythological name borne by the daughter of the legendary warrior Cairbre Nia Fer. She died of sorrow when the Ulster hero Conall Cearnach slew her brother and, according to legend, gave her name to the hill of Achall near Tara.

ACCOBRÁN: ACOBHRÁN (akav-rān) m, 'desirous'. The name of a saint of Kilrush, Co Clare, whose feast-day is 28 January. The name may be a translation of Latin *Desiderius*.

*ÁDAM: ÁDHAMH (āv, ā-ū) m.   The biblical Adam, borrowed first by clerics but later used more generally. Among others, the name was borne by the historian Ádam Ua Cianáin (†1373), and it gave rise to the Cork surname Ó hAdhaimh.

ÁDAMNÁN: ADHAMHNÁN (ū-nān) m, 'little Adam'. Generally anglicised *Eunan* or *Onan*. The best-known bearer of the name was Adamnán, abbot of Iona and author of a famous biography of St Colmcille, who died in 704. He is patron of the diocese of Raphoe and his feast-day is 23 September.

ADAMRAE: ÁMHRA (āv-ra) m, 'very wonderful'.   A very rare name which occurs in the early genealogy of the O Lohan (Loghan, Loughan, Duck) family of Westmeath.

*ADDUCC: ADAG (ad-ag) m, a diminutive of *Adam*. In thirteenth-century England Adam, with its diminutives *Add, Adkin, Atkin* etc., was one of the two or three most common names and, in its various forms, it became fairly common in Ireland as a result of the Norman invasion.

ADNACH: ADHNACH (ei-nach) m.   This name occurs in the early pedigrees of the leading Munster families, the Dál

Cais and the Eóganacht. It was also borne by a saint of the Airgialla who settled in Leittir Dalláin in Tír Eógain.

ADNÁR: ADHNÁR (ei-nãr) m, 'very modest'. The name of an early Leinster saint.

ÁED: AODH (ē) m, 'fire'. Cognate with Latin *aedes*, *aestus* and with the Gaulish *Aedui*, it was the commonest of all names in use in early Ireland and is now everywhere anglicised *Hugh*, a name with which it has no connection. Among the many kings and nobles who bore the name were Áed Sláne, high-king (†607), Áed mac Ainmerech, high-king who was slain by the Leinstermen in 601, Áed Allán, high-king (†613) and Áed Bennán, king of West Munster (†619), of whom the poet sang 'When he rattles his shield he scatters his enemies.' There were some twenty saints of the name among whom were St Áed mac Bricc of the royal race of the Southern Uí Néill, St Áed, bishop of Lisgoole, on Lough Erne, whose feast-day is 25 January and St Áed, bishop of Sletty, Co Carlow, who died in 699 and whose feast-day is 7 February. The name gave rise to a very large number of surnames, e.g. O Hea, Hayes, Hay, Hughes, McHugh, MacCue, McCoy, etc. In the form *Hugh* the name is still found in most Donegal families and there is scarcely a family of the O Donnells which has not a Hugh. The diminutive *Hughie* is very common in the north.

ÁEDAMMAIR: AODHAMAIR (ē-amir') f, derived from *Áed*. The name of a virgin saint whose feast-day is 18 January. The alternative form *Adamair* also occurs and this was the name of Guaire Aidne, king of Connacht.

ÁEDACH: AODHACH (ē-ach) m, derivative of *Áed*. A saint whose feast-day is 9 April.

ÁEDÁN: AODHÁN (ē-ān) m, diminutive of *Áed*. This was a relatively common name in early Ireland, both for clerics and laity. It was borne by some twenty-one saints among whom were St Áedán of Louth whose feast-day is 1 January, St Áedán, abbot of Lismore, whose feast-day is 16 March, and St Áedán of Aghara, near the river Inny in Roscommon, whose feast-day is 11 April. Perhaps the most famous bearer of the name was Áedán, the missionary sent by Iona to christianise the north of England and who founded the monastery of Lindisfarne. The name is commonly anglicised *Aidan* and *Edan* and was revived in England in the nineteenth century. In Ireland, *Aidan* is commonly used as a form of *Máedóc* (which see).

ÁEDGAL: AODHAL (ē-al) m. Meaning, perhaps, 'one possessing the prowess of (the god) Aed'. This early name is in use in the pedigrees of the Leinstermen and the Déisi.

ÁEDGEN: AOIDHGHEAN (ī-an) m. Meaning, perhaps, 'born of Aed' or 'born of fire'. Among the bearers of this name were St Áedgen, bishop and abbot of Fore, who died in 771 and whose feast-day is 1 May and Áedgen, bishop and scribe of Kildare(†865). The Old Irish name *Áedgna* is similar in formation and meaning.

ÁEDLUG: AODHLUGH, AOLÚ (ē-lū) m. A combination of *Áed* and the god-name *Lug*. This name was relatively common among the early inhabitants of Kerry. It was also borne by a saintly abbot of Clonmacnoise whose feast-day is 26 February.

ÁEDNAT: AODHNAIT (ē-nit') f, the female form of *Áedán* (above). It was borne by a St Áednait whose feast-day is 10 November. It is anglicised *Enat*, *Ena* and *Eny*.

ÁEDUCÁN: AODHAGÁN (ē-gān) m, diminutive of *Áed*. It is anglicised *Egan*. This name was widely used in early Ireland and gave rise to the surname Mac Aodhagáin (Mc Egan) — the outstanding legal family of medieval Ireland. It was also the name of the last great Munster poet Aodhagán Ó Raithile.

*AFFIATH m. The name of the biblical Japhet, one of the sons of Noah. It was borrowed by a number of early Irish clerics such as Affiath, abbot of Moville (†743), and Affiath, bishop of Armagh (†794), but it never became popular.

*AFFRAIC f. A borrowing of the name Africa. It was borne by two abbesses of Kildare in the eighth and ninth centuries. It was also the name of the daughter of Godred, King of the Isle of Man, who married John de Courcy and founded a Cistercian monastery in the Ards, Co Down.

ÁGACH: ÁGHMACH (āch) m, 'contentious, warlike'. The name of one of the Fomorians, legendary sea-borne raiders and enemies of the Tuatha Dé Danann.

ÁGDAE: ÁGHDHA, ÁGA (ā-ga) m, 'contentious, warlike'. A relatively rare name which occurs in the early pedigrees.

AÍ: AOI (ī) m and f, 'poetic inspiration, learning'. There was a legendary Aí mac Ollamon whose name means 'inspiration, son of master poet'. The best-known female bearer of the name was Aí Arduallach ('Aí the Arrogant'), daughter of Finn, who refused to marry the king of Scotland or any other man who was not Irish.

AÍBGRÉNE: AOIBHGRÉINE (īv-gr'ēn'e) f, 'radiance of the sun, ray of sunshine'. This name could be anglicised *Evegren*. In Irish saga she is the daughter of Noíse and the tragic heroine Deirdre.

AÍBELL: AOIBHEALL (ī-v'al) f, 'radiance, spark, fire'. One of the old Irish goddesses. According to some legends she is a supernatural lady who lives in the fairy-mound of Craig Liath near Killaloe, Co Clare, and who appeared to Brian Boru on the eve of the battle of Clontarf. In other stories there is mention of Aíbell, daughter of the Ulster warrior Celtchar mac Uithechair, and of Aíbell Grúadsolus ('Aíbell of the bright cheeks') who is daughter of the king of Munster. The name always retained its pagan associations.

AÍBINN, OÉBFINN, AÉBFHINN: AOIBHINN (ī-vin') f, 'beautiful sheen, fair radiance'. This name could be anglicised *Eavan*. It was borne by the mother of St Énna of Aran and by a number of princesses including the daughter of Donnchad, royal prince of Tara, who died in 952.

AÍBNAT, AÉBNAT, OÉBNAT: AOBHNAIT (īv-nit') f, 'radiant girl'. This name could be anglicised *Eavnat*. It was borne by a saint of Laois whose feast-day is 31 January.

AIBNE: AIBHNE (ev'-n'e) m. In the later middle ages this

15

name occurs among the Meic Lochlainn (McLoughlins) and Uí Chatháin (O Kanes) of Donegal and Derry. In more recent times, it was common among the O Kanes, O Brallaghans, Bradleys, Brodies and O Mullins of the same area. It has been anglicised *Eveny* and earlier *Aveny*.

AICCLECH: AIGLEACH (ag'l'ach) m. Meaning, perhaps, 'cautious, ready'. A rare name used among the early inhabitants of Kerry and Kilkenny.

AICHER: AICHEAR (e-har) m. Meaning, probably, 'sharp, keen, fierce'. The name was borne by one of the ancestors of the Uí Ógáin (Hogans) of Dál Cais. Aicher was also the ancestor of the Uí Aichir (O Hehirs) of Clare, most of whom came originally from Limerick. In the Finn-tales, Aicher is one of the musicians of the Fianna. The name could be anglicised *Ehir*.

AÍFE: AOIFE (ī-f'e) f, 'pleasant, beautiful, radiant (goddess)'. This ancient name, which the scholar T.F. O Rahilly associates with the Gaulish goddess, *Esuvia*, is borne by many of the legendary heroines of early Irish literature: Aífe, daughter of Belchú and wife of the Ulster hero Conall Cearnach; Aífe, daughter of Russ Failge and queen to a legendary king of Leinster; Aífe Foltfhind ('of the fair hair'), daughter of the king of Ulster; Aífe Derg, daughter of the King of Connacht who, according to story, had her marriage arranged by St Patrick himself. The name has been anglicised *Eva*, a name with which it has no connection.

AILBE: AILBHE (al'-v'e) m and f. Very probably connected with the old root *albho-* 'white' and with Gaulish *Albiorix* 'world-king'. Among the famous legendary and historic women who bore the name are Ailbe, daughter of the fairy king, Midir; Ailbe Grúadbrecc ('of the freckled cheeks'), daughter of Cormac mac Airt, who, according to the Fenian warrior Caílte, was one of the four best women of her time who ever lay with a man in Ireland; Ailbe, daughter of the high-king Máel Sechnaill I and mother of Cerball, warrior-king of Ossory. As a male name Ailbe occurs in both pagan and christian contexts. A legendary Ailbe of the Tuatha Dé Danann gave his name to a sea-inlet in Corcu Duibne.

Another is said to have voyaged in search of the Land of Promise. According to the Finn-tales twelve warriors of the Fianna bore the name Ailbe. There are two saints of the name, Ailbe mac Rónáin, a saint of Cenél Conaill, whose feast-day is 30 January and the much better known Ailbe, bishop of Emly, whose feast-day is 12 September. It is anglicised incorrectly as *Albert* and *Bertie*.

AILCHÚ (al'-chū) m.   Meaning, possibly, 'gentle hound'. This relatively uncommon name was borne by two eighth-century abbots, one of Clonard and one of Monasterboice. It also occurs among the Eóganacht pedigrees.

AILERÁN: AILEARÁN (al'-ar-ān) m.   A relatively rare name, the most famous bearer of which was Ailerán the Wise, a scholarly monk who wrote commentaries on the scriptures and who died in the great plague of 665.

AILGEL: AILGHEAL (al'-īal) m.   In the early period this was a relatively common name especially in the south of Ireland. From Ailgel of Dál Cais descend the O Duffs, O Dunnes, O Lynchs, O Deadys and O Cahills of north Munster.

ÁILGENACH: ÁILGHEANACH (āl'-īan-ach) m, 'soft, mild'. A rare early name.

ÁILGENÁN: ÁILGHEANÁN (āl'-an-ān) m, 'soft, mild person'.   This name occurs chiefly in the south and is borne by one of the early kings of Munster. It gives rise to the surname O Hallinan.

ÁILGESACH: ÁILGHEASACH, ÁILÍOSACH (āl'-īs-ach) m, 'desirous, eager, lustful'.   A north Munster name. It gives rise to the surname Ó hÁilgheasaigh (O Hallisey), which is now found almost exclusively in west Munster.

AILILL: OILILL (al'-il') m, 'a sprite, an elf'.   Perhaps the fourth most popular male name in early Ireland and now obsolete. Irish scholars latinised it *Elias* but it has no connection with this biblical name. The name is borne by both lay-folk and clerics. According to the Finn-tales, there were ten warriors of the Fianna who bore the name. Ailill, leader of a Connacht war-band, fought a battle with the legendary Fothad who had stolen his beautiful wife. Ailill Ólom ('Bare-ear'), according to the genealogical legends, is ancestor of all the leading royalty of Munster. There are two saints of the name, Ailill whose feast-day is 25 June and St Ailill, bishop of Armagh, whose feast-day is 13 January. Other notable bearers of the name were Ailill mac Cormaic, abbot and bishop of Slane (†802) and Ailill Ua Flaithim (Flahive), abbot of Ardfert and principal judge of Munster (†1032). Ailill was anglicised *Irial*, *Irrill* among the O Haras and O Garas in the seventeenth century and became *Oliver* among the O Haras.

AILILLÁN, AILILLÉN, AILELLÁN (al'-al-ān) m, diminutive of *Ailill*. A relatively rare name found in the early pedigrees of the Ulaid and Airgialla.

*AILIONÓRA (al'-an-ōra) f. This name was probably introduced to Norman England through Eleanor of Aquitaine (1122-1204), wife firstly of Louis VII of France and subsequently of Henry II of England. It became popular because Edward I married Eleanor of Castile (†1290). Norman influence introduced it to Ireland where, among others, it was borne by the daughter of the Earl of Kildare, wife of Conn Ó Néill, Earl of Tyrone (†1497) and by a daughter of the Earl of Desmond, wife of O Rourke (†1589). The normal English forms in use in Ireland are *Eleanor* and *Eleanora*.

AILITHIR: OILITHIR (ul'-i-hir) m, 'a pilgrim'. This is an exclusively clerical name in early Ireland. Among its bearers were St Ailithir the abbot whose feast-day is 7 January, St Ailithir of Muccinis on Lough Derg whose feast-day is 12 May, and St Ailithir of Clongesh, Co Longford, whose feast-day is 25 April.

AILLÉN, AILLÉNE, ELLÉN: OILLÍN (al'-īn', ul'-īn') m. Diminutive of *Ailill* (above) meaning 'little sprite, little elf'. The forms *Ailíne* and *Ailéne* also occur but these may represent a different name. The best-known Aillén is Aillén of the elfmound, the enemy of Finn, who burned Tara every *samain* with his fiery breath. Another Aillén issued from the elfmound of Cruachain and devastated Ireland.

18

AILLEANN (al'-an) f. This name was borne by the mother of the great northern king, Muirchertach mac Néill (†943) and by the mother of Tigernán Ua Ruairc, King of Breifne.

AINBERTACH: AINBHEARTACH (an'-v'art-ach) m. Perhaps 'doer of evil deeds'. A rare name which occurs among the early inhabitants of Kerry.

AINBTHECH: AINFEACH (an'-f'ach) m. Meaning, perhaps, 'stormy, tempestuous'.

AINBTHEN, AINBTHINE: AINFEAN (an'-f'an) f. Meaning, perhaps, 'storm, violence, fury'. This name was borne by a virgin saint whose feast-day is 2 January.

AINDER: AINNIR (an'-ir') f, 'a young woman'. In the Finn-tales Ainder is daughter of Barrán and wife of Caílte. There is also an early saint of the name.

AINDÍLES: AINNÍLEAS (an'-īl'as) m. Meaning, probably, 'a child of uncertain parentage, an adopted or affiliated child'. A name borne by the Uí Baígill (O Boyles), Uí Dochartaig (O Dohertys) and Uí Domnaill (O Donnells) in the fourteenth century.

ÁINDLE, ÁNLE: ÁINLE (ān'-l'e, an'-l'e) m, 'a hero, a champion, a warrior'. According to O Rahilly, the original meaning of this name was 'warm sunshine, fiery brightness', a by-name for the sun-god. The length of the first syllable is also in doubt and two names may have fallen together here. The most famous bearer of the name is Aindle, one of the three sons of Uisnech, who together with his brothers, eloped with Deirdre. The name was also borne by a scholarly monk of Terryglass.

ÁINE (ān'e), m and f, 'radiance, splendour, brilliance'. As a male name Áine occurred among the Ciarraige and other peoples but it became obsolete at a very early period. However, it retained its popularity as a female name. Áine is the goddess of the elfmound of Cnoc Áine (Knockainey, Co Limerick), daughter of the elfin Fer Í (Yew Man) and unwilling lover of the legendary Ailill Ólom (Bare Ear), ancestor of the Eóganacht. Aine was well known in Derry and Tyrone where, it was believed, she was a human woman spirited away at night from her husband's side. She was particularly attached to the Ó Corra (Corr) family, her descendants, and lamented their deaths most plaintively. The southern Áine was the *bean sidhe* of the Fitzgeralds. In other stories, Áine fell in love with the sea-god, Manannán mac Lir, who took her off to the Land of Promise. In the Finn-tales, Áine is the daughter of the king of Scotland who would sleep with no man in the world but Finn. Finn wooed and won her and she became mother of his two sons. There was also an early Leinster St Áine but little is known of her. By the end of the nineteenth century the name had been universally rendered *Hannah*, *Anna*, or *Anne*—a biblical name with which it has no connection whatever.

AINÉISLIS (an'-ēs'-l'is') m. Meaning, perhaps, 'careful, thoughtful'. This name is peculiar to the O Gradys, O Donovans, O Donnells and other north Munster and, on occasion, south Connacht families since the early middle ages. It is anglicised *Stanislaus* (a Slavonic name with which it has no connection) and *Standish*.

AINMERE: AINMIRE (an'-m'ir'e) m. Meaning, perhaps, 'great lord, leader' or 'wicked lord'. The most distinguished secular bearer of the name was Ainmere mac Sétnai (†569), an early high-king. There were two saints of the name St Ainmere, bishop and abbot of Rathnew, Co Wicklow, who died in 779 and whose feast-day is 2 November and St Ainmere of Aileach whose feast-day is 10 June. This name was anglicised *Anvirre* among the O Briens.

AIRARD, IRARD, URARD (ur-ard) m, 'very tall'. The best-known bearer of this name was Airard mac Coisse, chief poet of the Irish, who died in penitence at Clonmacnoise in 990.

AIRBERTACH: AIRBHEARTACH (ar'-v'art-ach) m, 'skilled, ingenious'. The most famous bearer of the name was the learned Airbertach mac Cosse, monastic scholar of Ros Ailithir (Rosscarbery) in the tenth century.

ÁIRDÍN (ār'-d'ín') m. A rare name in use among the

McRorys about Dungiven until the end of the nineteenth century. Perhaps a diminutive of *Artgal* or *Ardgar* (which see).

AIRECHTACH: OIREACHTACH (ir'-acht-ach) m.   Meaning, perhaps, 'having many followers'. A relatively common early Irish name especially in the south. From Airechtach of the royal dynasty of Connacht descend the well-known Connacht family Meg Oireachtaigh (Mac Geraghty, Geretty, Garrity).

AIRTTÍNE: AIRTÍN (art'-ín') m, a diminutive of *Art* (which see).

AISLINN (as'-l'in') f.   Perhaps identical with *aisling* 'a vision, a dream'. *Aislinge* occurs once as a male name in the early literature. Until the beginning of this century Aislinn was in use as a female name in Derry and Omeath especially among the O Kane and McCourt families. In Derry the name was anglicised *Elsha* and *Alice*, while in Omeath it became *Esther*.

*ALIS, AILIS (al'-is') f.   From Norman-French *Aliz*, a borrowing of German *Adalhaid* 'nobility'. By the twelfth century it had become very common in England and France and was brought into Ireland by the Normans. It is the equivalent of *Alice* and *Alicia*.

ALMU: ALMHA (al-va) f.   A lady of the Tuatha Dé Danann who, according to legend, gave her name to the fortress and hill of Almu in Leinster. This name has no connection with the English name *Alma*, which came into fashion after the battle of Alma in the Crimean war. It could be anglicised *Alva*.

ÁLMATH (ál-va) f.   A rare name borne by an early princess of Dál Riada in Ulster. It could be anglicised *Alva*.

*ALUSDAR, ALASTAR, ALUSDRANN (al-as-dar) m. A borrowing of the Greek name Alexander. Introduced to Scotland by Queen Margaret whose son was Alexander I of Scotland (†1124), it rapidly became popular. Contact between Scotland and Ireland brought it into the north of Ireland where it was very popular in Scoto-Irish families such as Meic Domnaill (MacDonnells), Meic Dubgaill (Mac'

Dowells) and others.

AMALGAID: AMHALGAIDH (āl-ī) m. A very old Irish name common especially in Munster and borne by one of the early kings of Munster. It was also borne by an early King of Connacht whose name is preserved in that of the barony of Tirawley, Co Mayo. There is also a St Amalgaid whose feast-day is 9 June. The name could be anglicised *Auley*. In the later medieval sources it is totally confused with *Amlaíb* (which see). *Awley* was very common among the Magawleys of Calry in the sixteenth century.

AMARGEIN: AIMIRGIN (av'-ir'-in') m, 'born of song'. According to legend, Amargein was the first poet of Ireland. In the legends of the jurists, Amargein passed the first judgment of the Irish. Another Amargein was poet to the Ulster heroes and brother-in-law of king Conchobar mac Nessa. The father of St Finnbar was Amargein. In the later middle ages it was a favoured name among the O Mores of Laois and occurred occasionally as a conscious revival among the learned family of O Clery.

*AMLAÍB: AMHLAOIBH (ow-liv) m. A borrowing of *Olaf* which is still a favourite name in all Scandinavian countries. It was brought to Ireland by the Viking invaders and adopted by the Irish. It became a favourite name among the Uí Donnchada (O Donoghues) of Loch Léin in the twelfth and thirteenth centuries, and from Amlaíb Mac Carthaig descend the Meic Amlaíb (Mac Auliffes), an important branch of the MacCarthys. It is still common in west Munster where however, it is absurdly anglicised as *Humphrey*, an Old English/Old German name with which it has no connection. It could more properly be anglicised *Auliffe* or *Olave*.

ANU: ANA (an-a) f, 'wealth, abundance'. According to O Rahilly, she was the Irish goddess of abundance. Her name is preserved in the place-name *Dá Chích Annan* 'the breasts of Anu', two breast-shaped mountains near Killarney. The tenth-century Irish scholar, Cormac, calls Anu 'the mother of the gods of the Irish'. The forms *Danu, Dana* seem to be later scholarly inventions. Despite its pagan associations, the name is also borne by the virgin St Ana whose feast-day is 18 June.

ANFUDÁN (an-fán) m.   Possibly meaning 'a turbulent, tempestuous fiery person'. The name was borne by an abbot of Linn Dúachaill who died in 763 and there is a St Anfudán, who was abbot of Glendalough and whose feast-day is 11 January. The name is obsolete since the early middle ages.

ANLÓN, ANLUAN (an-lūn) m.   Meaning uncertain, perhaps 'great hound, great warrior'. This name was borne by one of Brian Boru's ancestors and by his brother. In the north it gave rise to the well-known surname O Hanlon. It has been absurdly anglicised *Alphonsus* but it could more properly be rendered *Anlon*.

ANMCHAID: ANAMCHA (an-am-cha) m.   Native Irish scholars understood this name to mean 'spirited' and accordingly, translated it into Latin as *Animosus*. In the early period it was a relatively popular name especially in the southern half of Ireland. Anmchaid mac Murchada (†1017) was 'the chief poet of the south of Ireland'. Latterly, the name was much favoured by the O Maddens of Co Galway. Since the sixteenth century and perhaps earlier it has been equated with *Ambrose*, a name which has no connection whatever with it.

*ANNÁBLA, ANÁBLA: NÁBLA (an-āb-la) f.   A borrowing of the puzzling name Annabel(la), a name popular in Scotland since the twelfth century. It was introduced into Ireland by the Normans. In Omeath, it was re-anglicised *Mabel* in the nineteenth century while, in Donegal, the name reached a certain popularity under the form Nábla only to be turned again into *Mabel*. Mabel is a short form of *Amabel* which in all probability gave rise originally to Annabel(la).

*ANRAOI, ANNRAOI (own-rī) m.   A borrowing of the English name *Henry*, *Harry*, which was brought into Ireland by the Anglo-Normans. The form *Énri*, *Einri*, is also used. It became very common among the O Neills of Ulster. The first important O Neill to bear the name was Énri Aimréid (mac Néill Móir) who died in 1393 and after him the name achieved increasing popularity. In Derry and Omeath the name was pronounced *Yarry* at the beginning of this century.

ÁNROTHÁN (ān-ra-hān) m. The meaning is uncertain. O Rahilly argued that it meant 'the travelling sun', a by-name for the sun-god and, secondly, 'a champion, a hero', while Pokorny suggested that it meant 'a poet of the second grade' or 'a nobleman second only to the king'. In the form *Anroth*, the name occurs in the mythical portion of the Munster pedigrees. In the form *Ánrothán*, the name occurs in the Dál Cais genealogies and probably gave rise to the surname O Hanrahan. It could be anglicised *Anrahan*.

ÁRCHÚ (ār-chū) m, 'hound of slaughter'. A relatively uncommon early name.

ARÓC: ARÓG (ar-ōg) f. A name borne by the mother of the high-king Máel Sechnaill I (†862).

ARRACHTÁN (ar-acht-ān) m. Meaning, perhaps, a 'strong, vigorous or bold person'. In the early period it occurs as a name in the south of Ireland. It gives rise to the surname Ó hArrachtáin (Harrington).

ART (art) m, 'a bear'. This is the ancient word for a bear but it is never used except as a personal name or as a figurative word for 'a champion' in early Irish, for the bear is a taboo animal who is imagined as a destroyer or plunderer. The name is borne by many of the early legendary kings such as Art Óenfer ('the lonely'), father of Cormac mac Airt and Art Corb, legendary ancestor of the Déisi. The name retained its popularity down to modern times and was favoured by the MacMurroughs, Kavanaghs, O Connors, O Mulloys, O Rourkes, MacKiernans, O Haras, O Neills, O Keeffes and many other families. It was generally anglicised *Arthur* which, however, is incorrect for the two names have no connection with each other.

ARTÁN (art-ān) m, diminutive of *Art*. Though never widely used as a name, it gave rise to the surname Meic Artáin (MacCartan) of Down.

ARTGAL, ARDGAL, ARDGAR (ārd-al, ārd-gar) m. It is possible that here a number of different names have fallen together. If so, *Ardgar* is practically confined to the Mac Lochlainn dynasty in Ulster. *Artgal* probably means 'one who is fierce or valorous as a bear'. The name is relatively common in early Munster. As *Airdgal* it survived in east Ulster down to the beginning of the present century among the families of Mac Mahon, Mac Ardle, O Connelly, Mac Cabe and in some other Monaghan families. Among the Mac Mahons and McKennas of Ulster it was anglicised as *Arnold*, a Germanic name of totally different origin. *Áirdín* (which see) may be a diminutive.

ARTUCÁN: ARTAGÁN (art-ag-ān) m, a diminutive of *Art*. It gives rise to the surname O Hartigan and could be anglicised *Artigan*.

*ARTÚR (art-ūr) m.　A borrowing through British of the Latin name *Artorius*, identical with Arthur of the Arthurian literature. The earliest genuine reference to the name is that to Artúr, son of Áedán mac Cabráin, king of Scotland, who was slain in 596. Among early bearers of the name are Artúr mac Muiredaig, a petty king of Leinster, who died in 847 and Artúr, abbot of Clonmore (Rathvilly, Co Carlow), who died in 1052. Another Artúr of Dál Cais is ancestor of the Arthur family in Limerick. However, the name never became popular in Ireland and Irishmen who now bear the name either have it as an English borrowing or as a bad translation of *Art*.

ASSÍD: AISÍODH (as'-ī) m.　The name of one of the ancestors of the Meic Conmara (MacNamaras) who flourished in the tenth century. An ancestor of the Uí Rígbardáin (O Riordans) also bore the name. The name was also borne by Assíd mac Domnaill, king of Corcu Baiscind (in Co Clare) who died in 1049.

ATHCHE: AITHCHE (a-he) f.　Anglicised *Atty*. The name of a virgin saint of Cell Aithche, Co Limerick, whose feast-day is 15 January.

AUGAINE: ÚGHAINE (ū-n'e).　This name has been compared with Welsh *Owein*. Its principal (if not only) bearer was Augaine Mór, ancestor in prehistory of the Irish aristocracy.

AUGAIRE: ÚGHAIRE (ŭ-r'e) m. Meaning, possibly, 'shepherd'. This name was much favoured by a number of great Leinster families: Uí Nualláin (O Nolans), Uí Brain (O Byrnes), Uí Thúathail (O Tooles) and related families.

*AUGUSTÍN m. The name of Augustine, bishop of Hippo, or perhaps of Augustine, apostle of England, was borrowed on occasion by Irish clerics. Among its bearers were Augustín, abbot of Bangor, who died in 780 and Augustín Ua Cuinn, principal judge of Leinster, who died in 1095. It never spread widely. The forms *Arbhistín* and *Oistín* are in current use.

AURCHLOSSACH, URCHLOSSACH: IRCHLASACH (ŭr-chlas-ach) m. Meaning 'famous, reputable'. An early name found among the families of the Eóganacht, Ciarraige and Dál Cais.

AURTHUILE, ERTHUILE, AIRTHAILE (er'-hil'e) m. Meaning, perhaps, 'flood-tide, abundance, plenty'. A relatively common name in the very early period. It could be anglicised *Aurile*.

B

BACCÁN (bok-ān) m, 'little man'.   An early name in use among certain early Leinster peoples and a variant of *Beccán* (which see).

BÁETÁN, BAÍTÁN: BAODÁN (bēd-ān) m.   O'Brien considers this to be a borrowed name but it may equally be a pet-form of a compound name such as Báethgal, Báethgalach, Báethellach or some such. The name was relatively common in early Ireland. Among its bearers were the high-king Báetán mac Ninnedo (†586) and Báetán mac Cairill (†581), one of the most powerful of the kings of Ulster whom the early writers claim was king of Ireland and Scotland. There is also a St Báetán who was abbot of Clonmacnoise and whose feast-day is 1 March.

BÁETH, BAÍTH: BAOTH (bē) m, 'vain, reckless, wanton, foolish'.   A relatively common name in the very early pedigrees.

BÁETHÁN: BAOTHÁN (bē-hān) m, 'a vain, wanton, foolish person', diminutive of *Báeth* (above).

BÁETHGALACH: BAOTHGHALACH, BAOLACH (bē-he-lach, bē-lach) m, 'one capable of recklessness, of foolish valour'.   This early name became the special possession of the Mac Egans, O Dalys and a few other families in later times. It was latinised *Boethius* and it was anglicised *Bowes* among the O Dalys. It is more acceptably anglicised *Behellagh*.

BÁETHÍNE, BÁITHÍNE: BAOITHÍN (bī-hīn′) m, a diminutive of *Báeth* (above).   Among the bearers of this name are St Báethíne of Danganstown, Co Wicklow, whose feast-day is 22 May; St Báethíne, abbot of Iona and St Colm-cille's successor, whose feast-day is 9 June; St Báethíne, a bishop, who gave his name to Tibohine, Co Roscommon, whose feast-day is 19 February; and Báethíne, abbot of Birr, who died in 928.

BAÍGELL: BAOILL (bī-l) m. A relatively rare early Irish name which gave rise to the surname Uí Baígell (O Boyle), a distinguished Donegal family. The name could be anglicised *Boyle*.

BÁINE (bān′e) f, 'whiteness, paleness'. In the place-name legends Báine is the daughter of Frigrenn mac Rubai Ruaid, who gave his name to Ailech Frigrenn, now the great stone fortress of Greenan Elly in Donegal. In another legend, she is the daughter of Túathal Techtmar, ancestor of the kings of Ireland.

BAIRRE (bar′e) m, a pet-form of the names *Finnbarr* and *Barrfinn* (which see). It is generally anglicised *Barry*.

BAISCEND: BAISCEANN (bas′-k′an) m. Possibly meaning 'round head' or 'red head' but this is extremely uncertain. This very rare name was that of the ancestor of the Corcu Baiscind, an early Clare people. It was also borne by the tenth-century ancestor of the Baskin family. It could be anglicised *Baskin*.

BALLGEL: BAILLGHEAL (bīl′-al) f, 'bright limbed', 'white limbed'. Among the bearers of this name were a pious queen of Connacht, friend of St Mochua of Balla and, in the Finn-tales, a lady of the *sídh*, or elfmound, in Brega.

BANBA: BANBHA (ban-va) f. Originally this name was applied to the plain of Meath in which Tara lies but later it became another name for Ireland. It is also in use as a female name in the early mythology. Banba was the wife of Mac Cuill, one of the gods of the Tuatha Dé Danann.

BANBÁN: BANBHÁN (banv-ān) m, 'a piglet, a sucking-pig'. This name occurs especially in west Munster in the

28

early pedigrees. It was borne among others by two clerics, St Banbán whose feast-day is 9 May and Banbán, abbot of Clane, who died in 782.

BANBNAT: BANBHNAIT (banv-nit′) f, feminine form of *Banbán*. This name was borne by two early saints, one whose feast-day is 23 July and another whose feast-day is 11 August.

BARDDÁN, BARDDÉNE: BARDÁN (bard-ān) m, 'a poet'. This very old name is not very common in the early period but it did give rise to the surname Ó Bardáin (O Bardon, Barden, Bardane), a bardic family originally from Cos. Longford and Westmeath. It could be anglicised *Bardan*.

BARR (bar, bār) m, 'tip, point, top'.   A very rare early name.

BARRÁN (bar-ān) m, diminutive of *Barr*.   In the Finn-tales Barrán is the father of the wife of the warrior Caílte.

BARRDUB: BARRDHUBH (bar-uv) f, 'dark-headed, dark-haired'. This name was borne by the mother of a ninth-century king of Ulster and by a queen blessed by St Tigernach of Clones.

BARRFIND: BAIRRFHIONN, BAIRRIONN (bar′-in) m and f, 'fair-haired, fair-headed'. This is an exact equivalent of the Welsh name *Berwyn* or *Barwyn*. There are eight saints of the name including St Barrfhind, a Munster saint of the royal dynasty of the Eóganacht who settled on Little Island on the Suir near Waterford. Other lesser-known saints of the name have feast-days on 3 May, 21 May and 16 March. The best-known female bearer of the name was Barrfind, wife of a twelfth-century king of Ulster. The forms *Bairre*, *Barre* and *Barra* are pet-forms of this name and are anglicised *Barry*.

BÉBINN, BÉFIND: BÉIBHINN (bē-vīn′) f, 'white lady'. One of the more popular female names in early and medieval Ireland. A mythological Bébinn was wife of Áed Álainn ('the beautiful') and daughter of the king of the Otherworld. In saga, Bébinn is mother of the hero Fráech, the beloved of the women, who was slain by Cúchulainn. Other bearers of the name were Bébinn, wife of Tadc, King of Connacht

(†956), and Bébinn, daughter of Mac Con Caille, abbess of the nuns of Derry (†1134). The name continued in use throughout the later middle ages. On occasion it has been wrongly anglicised *Vivian*.

BÉ CHUILLE (bē chil′e) f. The daughter of Flidais, a legendary woman of the Tuatha Dé Danann.

BÉ FÁIL: BÉBHÁIL (b′ē-vāl′) f. Possibly meaning 'lady of Ireland'. This name was borne by the wife of the high-king, Donnchad mac Áeda, whose death is recorded in the annals in 801.

BÉ TÉITE: BÉTÉIDE (b′ē-tē-d′e) f. *Téite* means 'luxury' or 'wantonness' and the name may well mean 'wanton lady'. *Téite* (which see) is also a female name. Bé Téite was daughter of Flidais, a legendary lady of the Tuatha Dé Danann.

BECC: BEAG (b′ag) m and f, 'little, small'. Among the bearers of this name were Becc mac Dé, the prophet, and Becc, a female warrior who lived in Connacht.

BECCÁN: BEAGÁN (b′ag-ān) m, 'little man'. There were several saints of this name including St Beccán of Kilpeacon in Tipperary and in Limerick whose feast-day is 26 May and St Beccán of Emlagh, Co Meath. Frequently a pet form of the name, *Beccóc* or *Beagóg*, is used.

BECCNAT: BEAGNAIT (b′ag-nit′) f, 'little lady'. *Bicnead* is an alternative form of the name. Beccnat was the mother of St Finán Camm of Kinnitty.

BEIRGÍNE, BERGÉN: BEIRGÍN (b′erg′-īn′) m, 'a brigand, a robber, a soldier'. In the early period this name was found principally in the south of Ireland. It could be anglicised Bergin.

*BÉIRICHTIR: BEIRCHEART (b′er′-e-hart) m. The name of an Anglo-Saxon saint who settled in Tullylease, Co Cork, and who died in 840. His feast-day is 6 December. His name has been variously and wrongly anglicised *Benjamin*, *Ben*, *Bernard* and *Bertie*.

BEN LAIGEN: BEAN LAIGHEAN (b'an lein) f, 'lady of Leinster'. A later medieval name, it was borne by a daughter of O Donoghue of Loch Léin who died in 1261.

BEN MIDE: BEAN MHÍ (b'an v'í) f, 'lady of Meath'. This name was in use down to the seventeenth century and was borne by the womenfolk of O Connors, MacMahons, O Neills and others.

BEN MUMAN: BEAN MHUMHAN (b'an vūn) f, 'lady of Munster'. This name was in use down to the seventeenth century among the womenfolk of the O Connors, Mac Dermotts and others.

*BENÉN: BEANÓN (b'an-ōn) m. From Latin *Benignus* 'benign'. St Benén was the disciple of St Patrick. His feast-day is 9 November.

BÉOÁED: BEOAODH (b'ō-ē) m, 'living fire'. The principal bearer of this name was the sixth-century St Béoáed of Ardcarne whose feast-day is 8 March.

BÉOÁN (b'ō-ān) m, 'lively lad'. Béoán was fisherman to St Comgall. Another Béoán was father of St Mobí, and the father of St Ciarán of Clonmacnoise bore the same name. There is also a St Béoán whose feast-day is 26 October.

BEOLLÁN (b'ō-lān) m. A relatively rare name. Beollán of Dál Cais, who probably flourished in the tenth century, was ancestor of the Uí Beolláin (the modern Bolands) of Clare and Kerry.

BERACH: BEARACH (b'ar-ach) m, 'pointed, sharp'. Berach was a relatively common name in early Ireland. Of the saints of the name, one may mention St Berach, abbot of Bangor, whose feast-day is 21 April; St Berach mac Crimthainn whose feast-day is 18 November; and St Berach, abbot of Cluain Coirpthe and patron of Kilbarry, Co Roscommon. He was of the royal race of the Uí Briúin of Connacht and is patron of the O Hanlys. The O Hanlys continued to use Berach as a family personal name but in the nineteenth century they anglicised it *Barry*.

BERCHÁN: BEARCHÁN (b'ar-hān, b'ar-chān) m, diminutive of *Berach* (which see). This name was relatively popular in the early period. Among the saints of the name are St Berchán of Senchill (the present Dublin suburb, Shankill); St Berchán, the ancient patron of Glenbarhane (now Castlehaven), Co Cork; St Berchán of Eigg whose feast-day is 10 April; St Berchán, abbot of Glasnevin, whose feast-day is 12 October; St Berchán of Lough Erne whose feast-day is 24 November; and St Berchán, abbot and bishop of Clonsast in Offaly, whose feast-day is 4 December. The name could be anglicised *Barhan*.

BERRACH: BEARRACH (b'ar-ach) f. According to the Finn-tales, Bearrach Brecc ('the Freckled') was daughter of Cass of Cúailgne (Cooley) and was the most generous woman of her time in Ireland. She was third wife to Finn.

BICCSECH: BIGSEACH (b'ig-s'ach) f, 'little lady'. St Biccsech is patroness of Kilbixy and her feast-day is 28 June.

BIND, BINDE: BINN, BINNE (b'in'e) f, 'melodius, sweet, sweetness'. Bind, daughter of Modarn, is one of the fairy-women of Irish legend.

BLÁTH (blā) f, 'blossom, flower' or 'gentle, smooth'. There were two virgin saints of the name whose feast-days are 18 January and 28 January.

BLAT: BLAD (blad) m. This name is peculiar to the Dál Cais and other early dynasties which claimed kinship with them. Blad is an early ancestor of the O Briens, MacNamaras and related families.

BLÁTHÍNE: BLÁITHÍN (blā-hīn') f, 'flowerlet, blossom'. In the old tale of the death of the Munster warrior Cú Rói, the maiden who betrays him is Bláthíne, daughter of Conchobar. She was slain in vengeance by Cú Rói's poet. In the later stories she is called *Bláthnat* (which see).

BLATHMACC: BLÁMHAC (blā-vak) m, 'famous, renowned son'. One of the commoner names in early Ireland. Perhaps the best-known bearer of the name was Blathmacc, son of Áed Sláine, King of Ireland. Blathmacc mac Con Brettan was a superb early Irish religious poet. There is also a St

Blathmacc whose feast-day is 11 December.

BLÁTHNAT: BLÁTHNAIT, BLÁNAID (blā-nit') f, diminutive of *Bláth*, 'a flowerlet'. In later saga Bláthnat is the wife of the west Munster hero, Cú Rói. She fell in love with Cúchulainn and betrayed her husband by a stratagem. Cú Rói was slain but Cú Rói's poet, in vengeance for his death, seized Bláthnat and jumped from the cliff of Cenn Bera with her and both were killed. In religious legend St Brigit's cook is Bláthnat.

BLINNE (bl'in'e) f. A modern form of *Mo-ninne*, a virgin saint who was abbess and patroness of Killevy, Co Armagh. The name still survives in Omeath but it is anglicised *Blanche* — a name with which it has no connection.

BOAND: BÓINN (bō-n') f, 'cow-white (goddess)'. In Irish mythology Boand is the goddess of the Boyne, wife of the god Nechtain, and mother of Óengus, the young god.

BRAN (bran) m, 'a raven'. One of the most popular names in early Ireland and one favoured by the O Byrnes down to the end of the middle ages and later. According to the Finn-tales, there were two warriors called Bran in the Fianna. There is a St Bran associated with Clane, Co Kildare, whose feast-day is 18 May. One of the most famous kings of the Déisi was Bran Finn (†671), who was both a king and poet.

BRANACÁN: BRANAGÁN (bran-ag-ān) m, a diminutive of *Bran*. From this name comes the Cenél Eógain surname Ó Branagáin (O Branigan, Brangan).

BRANÁN (bran-ān) m, a diminutive of *Bran*. From Branán of Connacht descend the Meic Branáin (Mac Brannans), an important north Connacht family in the middle ages.

BRANDUB: BRANDUBH (bran-duv) m, 'raven-black'. A relatively common name in early Ireland. There are two saints of the name: St Brandub of Lough Ramor, near Virginia, whose feast-day is 6 February and St Brandub, a bishop, whose feast-day is 3 June.

BRECC: BREAC (br'ak) m, 'freckled, speckled'. This name was fairly widely used in early medieval Ireland especially in Munster where it gave rise to the surname Uí Bricc (O Brick), an important family among the Déisi. There is also St Brecc of the Déisi whose feast-day is 15 January.

BRECCÁN: BREACÁN (br'ak-ān) m, a diminutive of *Brecc*. The name was relatively common both as a clerical and lay name. There are some thirteen saints of the name of whom the best-known are Breccán of Dál Cais, who is associated with Aran and whose feast-day is 1 May; St Breccán of Kilkeel, Co Down, whose feast-day is 7 May; and Breccán, abbot of Moville, whose feast-day is 27 April.

BRECCNAT: BREACNAIT (br'ak-nit') f. Feminine form of *Breccán* and meaning 'freckled girl'. The feast-day of St Breccnat is 3 July.

*BRÉNAINN: BRÉANAINN (br'ēn-in') m. A borrowing of the Welsh word *breenhin* 'a prince'. The name was latinised *Brandanus*, *Brendanus*. The English form *Brendan* and the current Irish form Breandán are based on the Latin. The name was fairly widely used. There are seventeen saints of the name according to an early text. Of these the most important are St Brénainn of Fore whose feast-day is 27 July; St Brénainn of Birr whose feast-day is 29 November; and, the most famous of all, St Brénainn of Clonfert who was born in Kerry and is patron of the diocese of Kerry. The latter is also known as St Brendan the Navigator, the tale of whose voyages was translated into many languages in the middle ages. The female name *Brenda* is regarded in Ireland as a feminine from of Brénainn but it exists as an independent Shetland name deriving from the Norse name *Brand*. It has been suggested that its present popularity is due to its use by the novelist, Walter Scott, for one of the heroines of his novel, *The Pirate* (1821).

BRENDA: *See* Brénainn.

BRESLEÁN: BREASLÁN (br'as-lān) m, a diminutive of *Bressal* (which see). From this name derives the surname Ó Breasláin (O Breslin, Breslane), one of the more important medieval Irish legal families. The name could be anglicised *Breslin* or *Breslan*.

BRESS: BREAS (br'as) m. This name could mean either 'shapely, beautiful' or 'fight, uproar, din'. It is always borne by mythological or legendary characters in Irish literature. The most famous of these is Bress mac Elathan of the Tuatha Dé Danann.

BRESSAL: BREASAL (br'as-al) m, 'brave or strong in conflict'. This is a popular name in early Ireland and is especially common as the name of early kings. The most famous of these is Bressal Bélach, an early king of Leinster. The name is favoured by the O Kellys and the O Maddens of Connacht in the later middle ages. There is also a St Bressal whose feast-day is 18 May. It was anglicised *Brassal*, *Brissal*, *Bazil* and, on occasion, *Basil*.

BRESSALÁN: BREASALÁN (br'as-al-ān) m. A diminutive of Bressal which occurs occasionally.

BRIAN (br'ïan) m. The origin and meaning of this name present many difficulties. O Rahilly believes that it was borrowed on Irish soil from a population speaking a Celtic language like Welsh or British. The original form was *Brion* (two syllables which later developed into *Brian* with a new genitive, *Briain*). The original Celtic form is **Brigonos* (which gave the Irish name Bregon). If this is so, the original meaning of the word is 'high, noble'. The most famous bearer of the name – and the man responsible for its subsequent popularity – was Brian Boru, victor at the battle of Clontarf (1014) and ancestor of the Uí Briain (O Briens). Indeed, so much was the name associated with the O Briens that it never found any favour with their deadly enemies, the MacCarthys. The name was borne by many O Connors in the later middle ages and by their cousins, the mac Donaghs. The most famous O Neill to bear the name was Brian Catha an Dúna ('of the battle of Down'), who fell fighting the colonists at Downpatrick in 1260. It was also much used by the Mac Governs and the MacMahons of Ulster. The form *Brine* survived among the O Kellys of Omeath until the beginning of this century. Generally, it was anglicised *Bernard*, *Barnaby* and *Barney* in the course of the nineteenth century. An exactly similar name, *Brian*, was equally popular in England in the middle ages where it was introduced from Brittany. It gradually fell into disuse but survived in the north of England until the eighteenth century.

BRICCÉNE, BRICCÍNE: BRICÍN (br'ik-īn') m, a diminutive of *Brecc*, 'freckled, speckled'. According to the legends of the early Irish jurists, Cenn Fáelad, who first wrote down the Irish laws, was cured of his wound in the house of Briccíne of Túaim Drecon (Tomregan, Co Cavan). This Briccíne may be identical with St Briccíne of Tomregan whose feast-day is 5 September. The name was also borne by an abbot of Lorrha who died in 845. This name became obsolete at a very early period.

BRICCNE, BRICNE: BRICNE (br'ik'-n'e) m. A diminutive of *Brecc* which is used very rarely.

BRICCRIU, BRICCIRNE (br'ik-r'u) m. A very early derivative of *Brecc*. The only bearer of this name was Briccriu Nemthenga ('of the poison-tongue'), whose words set the men and women of Ulster quarrelling.

BRÍG: BRÍGH (br'ī) f. The original meaning of this word is probably, 'high, noble'. According to an Irish text, this name was borne by thirteen saints. These include St Brígh, a sister of St Breccán, of the royal dynasty of the Eóganacht of Cashel and St Brígh, a virgin saint of the Déisi, who lived near Lismore and whose feast-day is 31 January.

BRIGIT: BRIGHID, BRÍD (br'īd') f, 'the high goddess' from Celtic *Brigentí*. In the pagan Irish mythology Brigit is the goddess of poetry and mother of the three gods of craftsmanship, Brian, Liuchar and Uar. In a later tale, Brigit is the wife of Senchán Tairpéist, one of the almost legendary early poets. Ecclesiastical sources tell us that there were fifteen saints of the name Brigit. One of these, Brigit daughter of Cú Cathrach, had a church on the banks of the Shannon from which she sent gifts miraculously floating down the Shannon to St Senán of Inis Cathaig (Scattery Island), for Senán did not tolerate women on the island. The most famous of all these saints was, of course, St Brigit of Kildare, early patroness of the Leinstermen, whose feast-day is 1 February.

The name Brigit did not come into common use in Ireland until the modern period but as *Máel Brigte* 'devotee of St Brigit' and *Gilla Brigte* 'servant of St Brigit' it was much used in the medieval period. The name has been generally anglicised *Bridget* (which is properly the name of the Swedish St Brigitta, or Birgitta, who died in 1373, was canonised in 1391 and whose feast-day falls on 1 February). Other forms, pet-forms and equivalents are *Bride, Bryde, Breeda, Breetha, Bridie, Bidina, Dina, Bidelia, Delia, Dillie, Beesy, Biddy, Bid* and *Biddle*. In current usage, *Biddy* is the name for the stock Irishwoman of the lower class. *Brighdín, Brídín*, and *Bríde* are popular diminutives of Brigit.

BRION, BRIÓN (br'i-on, br'i-ōn) m.   For meaning, see *Brian*. The form *Brión* could be a diminutive of a name containing the word for 'high, noble'. Brion is relatively common especially in the very early period for legendary personages or founders of dynasties. The most famous bearer of the name was Brion, son of Echu Mugmedón, ancestor of the O Connors, O Flahertys, O Rourkes, O Reillys and many other noble Connacht families.

BRIÚINSECH: BRIÚINSEACH (br'ūn'-s'ach) f, a feminine form of *Brion* (which see). This was the name of the sister of St Mochua of Balla. It is also the name of a virgin saint whose feast-day is 29 May.

BROCC: BROC (bruk) m.   Perhaps 'a badger' or 'sharp-faced'. A relatively rare early name.

BROCCÁN: BROCÁN (bruk-ān), diminutive of Brocc.

BRÓCCÁN: BRÓGÁN (brōg-ān) m.   This is quite a common name in the early period especially in the south of Ireland. There are two saints of the name, St Bróccán mac Énna whose feast-day is 1 January and St Bróccán whose feast-day is 9 April. From this name comes the surname Ó Brógáin (O Brogan).

BRÓEN: BRAON (brēn) m.   This name which was relatively common in early Ireland was later confused with *Bran* (which see). It was borne by a number of early dynasts of Leinster and by St Bróen, a bishop of Cashel whose feast-day is 8 June.

BRÓENÁN: BRAONÁN (brēn-ān) m, a diminutive of *Bróen*. From this name comes the surname Ó Braonáin (O Brennan).

BROICSECH: BROICSEACH (brik-s'āch) f, feminine of *Broccán* (which see). This name was borne by the mother of St Senach of Cell Mór and by the mother of the great reformer and founder of the monastery of Tallaght, St Máel Ruain.

BRÓNACH (brōn-ach), m and f, 'sorrowful'. A rare early name.

BROINNFIND: BROINNINN (brin'-in') f, 'fair bosomed'. This was the name of the sister of St Ibar and mother of St Lithgen of Clonmore in Uí Failge.

BROTCHÚ (brut-chū) m. Meaning, perhaps, 'thieving hound, robber'. A name peculiar to the Uí Mathgamna (O Mahoneys) of Desmond in the twelfth century.

BRUATUR: BRUADAR (brūa-dar) m. O Rahilly declares that this name was borrowed on Irish soil from a language like Welsh. It was a relatively common name in the south of Ireland in the early period. It gives rise to the surname Ó Bruadair (Broder, Broderick).

BRUGACH: BRUGHACH (brūach) m. Meaning, perhaps, 'rich in lands' or 'rich in steadings'. This rare name was borne by a St Brugach whose feast-day is 3 November.

BRUINNECH: BRUINNEACH (brin'ach) f. *Bruinne* means 'bosom, breast' and, according to native scholars, *Bruinnech* is an old word for 'mother'. Bruinnech was a Munster princess whose virginity was miraculously restored by St Ciarán of Saigir.

BÚADACH: BUADHACH, BUACH (būach) m, 'victorious'. A favourite name among the Uí Suillebáin (O Sullivans) in the middle ages. It was translated *Boethius*. From this comes the surname Uí Buadaigh (Boohig, Booig) which is peculiar to Cork.

BÚADACHÁN: BUADHACHÁN, BUACHÁN (būach-ā) m, diminutive of *Búadach*. Búadachán was ancestor of the famous tenth-century king, Cellachán of Cashel, ancestor of the Meic Carthaig (Mac Carthys) and Uí Chellacháin (O Callaghans). The name gives rise to the surname Ó Buadacháin (O Bohan, Bohane, Buhan, Bohannon).

BÚADNAT: BUADHNAT, BUANAIT (būa-nit') f. Meaning, probably, 'victorious lady'. In the Finn-tales she is the daughter of the king of Norway.

BUAN (būan) m, 'lasting, enduring'. Buan belongs to the early Irish gods and is the ancestor of a number of early Irish tribes. The name never occurs outside mythological contexts.

BUANAND, BUANOND: BUANANN (būan-an) f, from *buan* 'lasting, enduring'. Buanand, according to the early Irish scholar Cormac, is 'the good mother who taught arms to warrior bands'. She is a goddess, mother of the *fían* and tutor in arms to Cúchulainn.

BUITE (buit'-e) m. This name was borne by St Buite mac Brónaig, founder of Monasterboice, whose feast-day is 7 December. A diminutive form *Buitén* occurs rarely.

C

CACHT (kocht) m and f, 'a slave, a bondmaid'. This early name is used principally as a female name but it also occurs as a male name.

CADAN: CADHAN (kein) m. A very early and rare name perhaps meaning 'a wild goose, a barnacle goose'. In the legends of Derry, Cadan and his wonderful hound killed a *piast*, or monster, in Gleann Chon Chadhain. It gives the modern surname Ó Cadhain and could be anglicised *Kyne*.

CADLAE: CADHLA (kei-la) m, 'beautiful, comely'. This name occurs among the Dál Cais and other Munster peoples. It gives the surname Ó Cadhla and could be anglicised *Kiely*. It has been latinised *Catholicus*.

CÁECHÁN: CAOCHÁN (kēch-ān) m, 'purblind, dim-sighted'. An uncommon name which gives the Clare surname Mac Caogháin (Keehan).

CÁEL: CAOL (kēl) m, 'slender, fine, thin'. In the early period this name is found principally in the south. It was borne by one of the heroes of the Finn-tales who was slain at the battle of Ventry.

CÁELÁN: CAOLÁN (kēl-ān) m, 'slender lad'. As well as being a secular name, this name was borne by two saints, St Cáelán whose feast-day is 30 June, and St Cáelán of Inis Celtra (Holy Island on Lough Derg), whose feast-day is 29 July.

CÁELBAD, CÓELUB: CAOLBHADH (kēl-va) m. A fairly

40

common name in the very early and legendary period, it was also the name of a saint whose feast-day is 21 August.

CÁELFIND, CÁELAINN: CAOILAINN (kēl-in´) f, 'slender, fair (lady)'. The best known bearer of this name was St Cáelainn, a virgin saint of the Ciarraige in Connacht, whose feast-day is 3 February.

CÁELCHÚ: CAOLCHÚ (kēl-chū) m, 'slender hound, warrior'. This name war borne by the patron-saint of Magheracloone, Co Monaghan, whose feast-day is 24 September.

CÁELTIGERN: CAOILTIARN (kīl´-t´īarn) f, 'slender lady'. This name was borne by the niece of St Kevin (Cáemgen) and mother of St Dagán.

CÁEM: CAOMH (kēv), m, 'precious, beloved, beautiful'. The principal bearer of this name was Cáem, ancestor of the Uí Chaím, the present-day O Keeffes.

CÁEMÁN: CAOMHÁN (kēv-ān) m, 'beloved person, friend'. This name was borne by three saints; St Cáemán, whose feast-day is 14 March, St Cáemán whose feast-day is 18 March, and St Cáemán of Ardcavan, near Wexford, whose feast-day is 7 June.

CÁEMELL, CÁEMGEL: CAOIMHEALL (kīv´-al) f. From *cáem* 'beautiful, beloved'. This name was borne by the mother of St Kevin (Cáemgen), by the abbess of a nunnery near Lismore, and by the mother of St Senán of Inis Cathaig (Scattery Island).

CÁEMFIND: CAOIMHINN (kīv-in´) f, 'beautiful and fair'. This was the name of the daughter of Conall Echlúath, legendary ancestor of the O Briens and related families.

CÁEMGEN: CAOIMHÍN (kīv´-īn´) m, 'beautiful birth, comely child'. The principal bearer of this name was St Cáemgen (Kevin), abbot and founder of Glendalough, whose feast-day is 3 June. There is another saint of the name whose feast-day is 11 May. The name has been anglicised *Kevin*.

CÁEMLUG: CAOMHLÚ (kēv-lū) m, from *cáem* 'beautiful, beloved' and the god-name, Lug (which see). This was the name of the father of St Cáemgen (Kevin) of Glendalough.

CÁEMNAT: CAOMHNAIT, CAOMHNAD (kĕv-nit′) f, 'beautiful girl'. This name was borne by two early female saints, one whose feast-day is 23 August and another whose feast-day is 24 April.

CÁEMÓC: CAOMHÓG (kĕv-ōg) f, 'beautiful, beloved girl'. A relatively rare name borne by an early Leinster saint.

CAICHER: CAICHEAR (ko-her) m. In the early period, this relatively uncommon name is found mostly in north Munster and south Connacht. It was the name of the druid of one of the legendary conquerors of Ireland but it was used also in Christian Ireland and was borne, for example, by Caicher mac Máenaig, abbot of Mungret, who died in 1007.

CAILLÉNE: CAILLÍN (kal′-īn) m. The most famous bearer of this name was St Caillín, bishop of Fenagh, whose feast-day is 13 November. The early prince, Cailléne Dub, was ancestor of the kings of Uí Liathain, an early and important kingdom in east Cork.

CAILTE, CAÍLTE: CAOILTE (kīl′-t′e) m. O Rahilly maintains that there are two separate names here. The first, Cailte, he takes to mean 'hard' and was borne by Cailte Bolg, ancestor of the people of Ossory. The second, Caílte, is the name of Caílte mac Rónáin of the Finn-tales, a warrior noted for his swiftness of foot. However, it is doubtful if there is any difference between the two. The name remained in use until the ninth century.

CAIMMÍNE: CAIMÍN (kom′-īn′) m. From *cam* 'stooped, bent'. This name is found more usually in the south. Its most famous bearer was St Caimmíne, abbot of Inis Celtra (Holy Island on Lough Derg), who died in 654 and whose feast-day is 25 March.

CAÍMSECH: CAOIMHSEACH (kīv′-s′æch) f, 'beautiful, beloved girl'. This name was borne by a female saint of Connacht whose feast-day is 30 November.

CAÍNDELBÁN: CAOINLEÁN (kīn′-lan) m, 'of beautiful

shape'. Caíndelbán mac Máel Chróin was ancestor of the well-known Uí Néill family Uí Chaíndelbáin (Kindellan). The name could be anglicised *Quinlan* or *Quinlevan*.

CAINDER: CAINNEAR (kon'-er) f. In legend, Cainder is daughter of Medb (Maeve), queen of Connacht. Of the Christian saints of the name the most important are St Cainder of Old Kilcullen, in the vale of the Liffey, and patroness of the area around Fore, in Meath, whose feast-day is 28 January; St Cainder of Abbeylara, Co Longford; and St Cainder, mother of St Mochua of Clondalkin, whose feast-day is 6 August. There is also a rare male name *Caindir* but this may be of different origin.

CAINNECH: CAINNEACH, COINNEACH (kon'-ach) m and f. This occurs as a female name amongst the southern Uí Néill. Cainnech, daughter of the high-king, Donnchad mac Flaind, died in 929. It was more common, however, as a male name, both for laymen and clerics. There were four saints of the name, the most important being St Cainnech of Aghaboe whose feast-day is 11 October and who is patron of Kilkenny. The name has been anglicised *Canice* and, less commonly, *Kenny*.

CAINNECHÁN: CAINNEACHÁN (kon'-ach-ān) m. A rare diminutive of *Cainnech* (which see).

CAINNLECH: CAINNLEACH (kon'-l'ach) f. Meaning, perhaps, 'shining, lustrous'. Cainnlech, daughter of Gamgelta, was foster-mother of the Ulster hero Cormac Connloinges. She died of sorrow, according to saga, when her beloved foster-son was slain.

CAÍNTIGERN: CAOINTIARN (kin'-t'iarn) f, 'gentle lady'. The most famous bearers of this name were Caíntigern, wife of Fiachna mac Báetáin, king of Ulster (†626) and mother of the hero Mongán, and Caíntigern, wife of Cellach Cualann, king of Leinster (†715).

CAIRBRE (kar'br'e) m. Perhaps the sixth most popular name in early Irish society. The most famous legendary bearer of the name was Cairbre Lifechair ('Liffey-lover'), son of Cormac mac Airt. Cairbre, son of Niall of the Nine

Hostages, was founder of a royal dynasty and gave his name to the barony of Carbury, Co Kildare. In early legend, Cairbre Músc is ancestor of the Múscraige (people of Muskerry). Of the Christian saints of the name the most important are: St Cairbre, bishop of Moville, whose feast-day is 3 May; St Cairbre, bishop of Assaroe, whose feast-day is 1 November; and St Cairbre whose feast-day is 6 March. The name was in use among the O Connors of Connacht in the fifteenth century and it died out in Ulster only in the late nineteenth century.

CAÍRECH: CAÍREACH (kīr′-ach) f. The most important bearer of this name was St Caírech Dergáin of Clonburren on the banks of the Shannon whose feast-day is 9 February. She was the special patroness of the women-folk of the O Kellys, O Maddens, O Mulallys and other families of Uí Maine in Connacht.

CAIRELL: CAIREALL, COIREALL (kor′-al) m. In the early period, this name is found chiefly in the north. There were nine saints of the name the most important being the saintly bishop, Cairell, whose feast-day is 13 June. This name could be anglicised *Kerill*. In recent times, it has been used as an Irish form of the Greek name *Cyril*, which became popular in England in the nineteenth century.

CAIRELLÁN: CAIREALLÁN (kor′-al-ān) m. A diminutive form of *Cairell* which gave rise in the north to the surnames O Carolan and Carleton.

*CAIRENN: CAIREANN (kar′-an) f. A borrowing from Latin *Carina*. The only bearer of this name was Cairenn Chasdubh ('of the dark curly hair'), daughter of the king of the Britons and mother of Niall of the Nine Hostages, legendary ancestress of the high-kings of Ireland.

CAIRNECH: CAIRNEACH (kar′-n′ach) m, 'cleric, tonsured one'. There were two saints of the name: bishop Cairnech whose feast-day is 28 March and St Cairnech, a Briton from Cornwall, who settled at Tuilen near Kells and whose feast-day is 16 May.

CÁIRTHENN: CÁIRTHEANN (kār′-han) m. A relatively

common name in the early period especially in the south where it occurs among the legendary ancestors of the O Briens and related families.

CAISSÉNE, CAISÍN (kos'-īn) m and f. Probably from *cas* 'curly-haired'. The most important bearer of this name was Caissíne mac Cais, legendary ancestor of the MacNamaras, O Gradys, O Hickeys, O Sheedys, Clancys and other Clare families. It occurs as a female name in the twelfth century.

*CAITERÍNA: CAITRÍONA, CATRAOINE (kot'-r'in-a) f. This is a borrowing of *Catherine*, the name of a virgin-martyr of Alexandria (†307) whose legend was brought into the west by the crusaders. The name became popular in Ireland through Norman and English influence and was well-established among the Irish aristocracy by the fifteenth century. The Old French forms *Caterine* and *Cateline* gave rise to the Irish forms *Caitríona* and *Caitilín* (Caitlín). Common abbreviated and pet-forms are *Cáit*, *Cáitín*, *Tríona*, *Traoine*, *Ríona*. The name has been translated into English as *Kathleen*, *Kate*, *Katie*, *Kathy*, *Kitty* and *Kay*.

CALBHACH, CABHLACH (kol-vach) m, 'bald'. This name was common in the later middle ages especially among the O Connors, O Carrolls, O Reillys, O Donnells and other families. It was anglicised as *Charles* among the O Connors and other families. *Calvagh* is a more acceptable English form.

CANACÁN: CANAGÁN (kon-ag-ān) m, a diminutive of *Cano* 'wolf-cub' (which see). A very rare early Irish name.

CANANNÁN (kon-an-ān) m, a diminutive of *Cano* 'wolf-cub' (which see). This early Irish name is apparently found only in the north.

CANAIR (kon-ir') f. Perhaps a variant of *Cainder* (which see). The most famous bearer of the name was Canair the Pious, a holy woman of Bantry who came to St Senán of Inis Cathaig (Scattery Island) requesting that she be buried on the island. 'Women enter not this island', said Senán. She replied: 'Christ came to redeem women not less than to redeem men' — and won her point.

CANO: CANA (kon-a) m, 'wolf-cub', figuratively 'a young warrior'. The most famous bearer of the name is Cano mac Gartnáin, a seventh century Scoto-Irish king who took refuge in Ireland and who, in story at least, was the lover of the lady Créd.

CARTHACH (kor-hach) m, 'lover, loving person'. A relatively common early Irish name which is found especially in the south. The most famous secular bearer of the name was Carthach mac Saírbrethaig, ancestor and eponym of the MacCarthys. There were two saints of the name, St Carthach, bishop and fosterson of St Ciarán of Seir, whose feast-day is 5 March; and St Carthach (also known as St Mochuda) founder of the famous monastery of Lismore whose feast-day is 14 May. The name has been anglicised *Carthage*.

CASS: CAS (kos) m, 'curly-haired'. A relatively popular early Irish name, the most famous bearer being Cass, legendary ancestor of the Dál Cais (O Briens, MacNamaras, O Gradys and others). There was also a St Cass of Bangor whose feast-day is 26 April.

CASSAIR (kos-ir') f. Perhaps from *cass* 'curly-haired'. According to the legends of the saints, Cassair, a holy virgin who was daughter of Áed, on seeing St Kevin's ragged rough clothes, begged him in the name of the Lord to wear something better. But Kevin refused. She was saddened by this but was so impressed that she placed herself and her convent of nuns under his rule.

CASSÁN (kos-ān) m, from *cass* 'curly-haired'. There are two early saints of the name, one whose feast-day is 4 June and another whose feast-day is 19 June.

CATHACH (ko-hach) f, 'warlike'. In legend Cathach Chatutchenn was a female warrior who loved Cúchulainn the hero of the Ulstermen.

CATHAÍR: CATHAOIR (ko-hīr) m. O Rahilly believed that this name meant 'battle-lord' but other scholars consider that it is a borrowing from some language unknown to us. The most famous bearer of the name was Cathaír Már, legendary ancestor of the Leinstermen who, in story at least, had thirty-three sons and reigned over Leinster for fifty years. In the later middle ages it was a particularly favoured name by the O Connors of Offaly, O Byrnes of Wicklow, O Dohertys and O Gallaghers of Donegal and, to a lesser degree, by the MacClancys, O Rourkes, O Reillys and others. *Cathair* is a by-form of the name in Donegal where, perhaps, it survived longest. It was everywhere anglicised *Charles*. The earlier English form *Cahir* is more acceptable.

CATHAL (ko-hal) m, 'strong in battle'. One of the most common names in Ireland in the early middle ages. Amongst its most famous bearers were Cathal mac Finguine (†742), one of the most powerful early kings of Munster and Cathal Crobderg ('of the Wine-red Hand'), king of Connacht (†1224). It was a favourite name among the O Connors of Connacht throughout the medieval and early modern period and was also much used by the MacManuses, Maguires, MacDonaghs and other families. It was everywhere anglicised *Charles* — a name with which it has no connection whatever.

CATHALÁN (ko-hal-ān) m. A diminutive of *Cathal* (which see). An early name found mostly in the south. It could be anglicised *Cohalan*.

CATHÁN (koh-ān) m. Derived from *cath* 'a battle' and, perhaps, meaning 'battler'. This name was particularly favoured in Munster among the Dál Cais and other inhabitants of west Munster while in the north it gave the surname Ó Catháin (O Kane), the name of one of the most prominent Ulster families down to the plantation. There was also a St Cathán of the Dál nAraide of Antrim.

CATHASSACH: CATHASACH (koh-as-ach) m, 'vigilant in war'. A relatively common name in the very early period. Among those who bore it was Cathassach mac Guasáin, scholar of Armagh, who died in 947. It gives rise to the surnames Mac Casey and O Casey.

CATHBARR: CATHBHARR (ko-far) m. Meaning, perhaps, 'protector'. This very early name occurs in Ogam inscriptions but in later times it was especially favoured by the

O Donnells and other northern families. It has been anglicised *Caffar*.

CATHCHERN (koh-ern) m, 'battle-lord'. This very rare early name could be anglicised *Cohern*.

CATHGAL: CATHAÍL (koh-íl′) m, 'fierce in battle, able for battle'. A relatively rare early name which occurs among the Dál Cais and other families.

CATHMÁEL: CATHMHAOL (koh-vēl) m, 'battle-champion'. An uncommon early name.

CATHNIO: CAITHNIA (koh-n′ia) m, 'battle-champion'. A relatively popular name in early Irish society.

CATHRAE: CATHRA (koh-ra) m. Various derivations have been suggested for this very early name. The most acceptable is that of Pokorny, 'battle-king'. It may, however, be confused with another name *Cathrua* which means 'battle-champion, warrior'.

*CAUSANTÍN: CONSALDÍN, CANSAIDÍN (kow-sad′-ín′) m. A borrowing of Latin *Constantinus* from *constans* 'constant, faithful'. It is found chiefly in the north and in Scotland where it was borne by four early Scottish kings. It was also borne by a twelfth-century nobleman-bishop of Killaloe who is the ancestor of the modern Considines.

CÉIBHFHIONN: CÉIBHIONN (kēv′-un) f, 'lady of fair locks'. In Irish mythology, Céibhfhionn was daughter of Becc mac Buain of the fairy-mound of Cahirnarry.

CELLACH: CEALLACH (k′a-lach) m and f. Traditionally believed to mean 'frequenter of churches', it is almost certainly a much older name meaning 'bright-headed'. A text of the Old Irish period says that this name may be male or female. It was, in fact, borne by the daughter of Donnchad, king of Uí Liatháin in east Cork, who died in 732. However, it was much more common as a male name and gave rise to the surname Ó Cellaig (O Kelly). Amongst its bearers were St Cellach mac Condmaig, abbot of Armagh, whose feast-day is 1 April; St Cellach, deacon of Glendalough, whose feast-day is 7 October; and Cellach Ua Máel Corgais, principal poet of Connacht, who died in 1000. It has been rendered *Celsus* in Latin and English.

CELLACHÁN: CEALLACHÁN (k'al-ach-ān) m, a diminutive of *Cellach* (which see). This name was particularly favoured by the MacCarthys, O Callaghans, O Herlihys and related families. Common in the twelfth century, it reappears in the sixteenth and seventeenth centuries and is still in use among the same families. There is an early St Cellachán whose feast-day is 22 April. It is anglicised *Callaghan*.

CELLSACH: CEALLSACH (k'-al-sach) f. A feminine form of the relatively rare male name *Cellán*, which is probably a diminutive of *Cellach* (which see). The most important bearer of this name is St Cellsach, a female saint of Muskerry, who settled on the banks of the Munster Blackwater.

CENNÉTIG: CINNÉIDE (k'in'-ēd-ig') m, 'ugly-headed, rough-headed'. In the early period, this name was found principally in the south. It was borne, among others, by Cennétig mac Gaíthíne, king of Laígis and famous battler against the Vikings, and by Cennétig mac Lorcáin, king of Dál Cais and father of Brian Boru. It gives the modern surname Ó Cinnéide (O Kennedy) and, as a personal name, is still in use and has been anglicised *Kennedy*.

CENN FÁELAD: CIONNAOLA (k'in-ēla) m, 'wolf-head'. This name was very common in the early period. Amongst its bearers was Cenn Fáelad father of St Íte of Limerick; St Cenn Fáelad, abbot of Bangor, whose feast-day is 8 April; and Cenn Fáelad Ua Cuill (O Quill), principal poet of Munster, who died in 1048. In the legends of the early Irish lawyers, Cenn Fáelad, son of Ailill, was wounded at the battle of Moira and lost his 'brain of forgetfulness'. As a result, what he learned in the law school by day he remembered and wrote down at night and to him is attributed the earliest written record of Irish law. This name gives the modern surname Ó Cionnaola (O Kennelly) and could be anglicised *Kennelly*.

CENNSELACH: CINNSEALACH (k'in'-s'al-ach) m, 'overbearing, proud, masterful'. The most famous bearer of this name was Énna Cennselach, legendary ancestor of the royal dynasty of south Leinster and of the families of MacMurrough, Kinsella, Maddock, Murphy and others. It could be anglicised *Kinsella*.

CERA: CEARA (k'ar-a) f. Meaning, perhaps, 'red, bright red'. Cera was one of the wives of Nemed, legendary invader of Ireland, who, according to medieval scholars, gave her name to Mag Cera (Carra), Co Mayo. There were also three virgin saints of the name whose feast-days fell on 5 February, 8 February and 9 September.

CERBALL: CEARBHALL, CEARÚL (k'ar-ūl) m. Meaning, perhaps, 'brave in sword-fighting, valorous in battle'. This much favoured early Irish name was borne by such persons as Cerball mac Dúngaile, king of Ossory (†888), one of the great warrior-kings of the Viking period; Cerball mac Muiricán, king of Leinster (†909); and by many of the early Leinster aristocracy. In the later middle ages, it was favoured by the learned family of Ó Dálaigh (O Daly). It has been wrongly anglicised *Charles*.

CERNACH: CEARNACH (k'ar-nach) m, 'victorious, triumphant'. Much favoured in the early period, this name later fell into disuse. Perhaps its most famous bearer was Cernach Sotal ('the Arrogant'), son of the high-king Diarmait (†665), who was so called 'for his pride and high spirits', says an early writer.

CÉTACH: CÉADACH (k'ēd-ach) m. Possibly a pet-form of a longer name containing the element *cét* 'first' or derived from *cét* 'a hundred', meaning somebody who counted his wealth in hundreds. It was borne by one of the sons of Cathaír Mór, legendary ancestor of the Leinstermen. In the later middle ages, it was favoured by the O Mores, O Farrells and other families. It has been anglicised *Kedagh*.

CETHERN: CEITHEARN (k'eh-arn) m. Meaning, perhaps, 'long-lived, lasting'. According to O Rahilly, this was another name for the god of the Otherworld. In Irish mythology, Cethern is father of the famous druid Mug Roith. Cethern is also another name for the father of the god Lug.

CETT: CEAT (k'at) m, 'old, ancient, enduring'. Its most famous bearer was the incomparable early warrior Cett mac Mágach of the *Táin*. Cett mac Flaithbertaig was king of Corcu Modruad (Corcumroe) in the tenth century and the name was particularly favoured by some Clare families.

CIAN (k'ĭan) m, 'ancient, enduring'. This name was borne by two legendary heroes, Cian Cúldub ('of the Dark Hair') of Leinster and Cian, son of Ailill Ólom, ancestor of the Cianachta peoples. Until the nineteenth century it was in use among the O Haras and Ọ Garas, who traced their descent from Cian, son of Ailill Ólom, but they anglicised it as *Kean* and, more rarely, *King*. The name was also borne by Cian mac Mael Muad, son-in-law of Brian Boru and ancestor of the O Mahoneys, who was slain at the battle of Clontarf in 1014. Ever since, it has been a favoured name among the O Mahoneys who, however, anglicised it absurdly as *Cain* in the nineteenth century.

CIANÁN (k'ĭan-ān) m, diminutive of *Cian* (which see). There were two saints of this name, St Cianán the abbot, whose feast-day is 25 February and St Cianán, bishop and founder of Duleek, whose feast-day is 29 November.

CIAR (k'iar) f, 'dark, black'. The most important bearer of this name is St Ciar, virgin patroness of Killkeary (Cell Cére) near Nenagh, whose feast-days are 5 January and 16 October.

CIARÁN (k'ĭar-ān) m, from *ciar* 'dark, black'. According to early Irish sources, there were some twenty-six saints of the name. The best known of these are St Ciarán, founder of Clonmacnoise, whose feast-day is 9 September; St Ciarán the Elder of Seir (also much venerated in west Cork) whose feast-day is 5 March; St Ciarán of Clonsast whose feast-day is 30 April; and St Ciarán of the vale of the Newry river whose feast-day is 4 February. Ciarán never became common as a secular name in the early period. It has generally been anglicised *Kieran*.

CIARMACC: CIARMHAC (k'ĭar-vok) m, 'dark son'. A not very common name which occurs principally in the south in the early period. It gives the Munster surname Ó Ciarmhaic, now rendered *Kirby*.

CIARNAT: CIARNAIT (k'īar-nit') f, 'dark lady'. This is the female form of *Ciarán*, the most famous bearer of the name being Ciarnat, mistress of the legendary king, Cormac mac Airt.

CILLÉNE, CILLÍNE: CILLÍN (k'il'-īn') m. Perhaps derived from *cell* 'a church, cell'. Among the many saints of this name were St Cillíne ua Colla, abbot of Fahan, Co Donegal, whose feast-day is 3 January; St Cillíne of the Déisi, whose feast-day is 26 March; St Cillíne the bishop of Tallanstown, near Ardee, whose feast-day is 27 May; and St Cillíne Droicthech, abbot of Iona, whose feast-day is 3 July. It is anglicised *Kilian*.

*CINÁED, CINÁETH: CIONAODH (k'un-ē) m. This name is certainly a borrowing into Old Irish and may well be Pictish in origin. It was borne by the high-king, Cináed mac Irgalaig (724-28) and appears to have become popular in Ireland after his time. It was also borne by Cináed mac Ailpín (†860), the first king of Scotland. Cináed úa hArtacáin was one of the best known of the early medieval Irish poets (†975). The name has been anglicised *Kenneth*, both in Ireland and in Scotland, and has achieved a considerable popularity.

CITHRÚADH: CIOTHRUADH (k'i-rua) m. This was a very common name among the learned families of O Duigenan and Mac Firbisigh. It was anglicised *Kihrooe* and transformed into *Jerome* in the seventeenth century.

CLÉIRECH: CLÉIREACH (kl'ēr'-ach) m, 'clerk, cleric'. This name was relatively common among clerical and learned families and gave rise to the surname Ó Cléirigh (O Clery).

CLÉRCHÉNE: CLÉIRCHÍN (kl'ēr'-hīn') m, diminutive of *Cléirech*. This relatively rare early name gave rise to the surname Clerkin (Clarkin).

*CLEMENS m. This was the name of a saintly disciple of St Paul and was borne by many popes. It was borrowed into Irish by the christian clergy and occurs occasionally among clerical and learned families from the ninth to the fourteenth century.

CLÍDNA: CLÍODHNA (kl'í-na) f. Clídna belonged to the Tuatha Dé Danann and in legend gave her name to one of the three great waves of Ireland, *Tonn Chlídna*, which has been identified with Glandore Harbour. In the Finn-tales, Clídna is one of the three beautiful daughters of Libra, poet to the sea-god Manannán mac Lir. In later legend, she is fairy-woman to the MacCarthys.

CLODAGH f. This is the name of a river in Tipperary (and of a number of other Irish rivers) and was first given as a christian name to the daughter of the Marquis of Waterford, after which it became popular. The Irish form of the river-name is *Clóideach*, the more common English form being *Clodiagh*.

CLOTHACH (klo-hach, klōch) f, 'famous, renowned'. In Irish mythology Clothach is grandson of the Dagda, the Good God. There is also a Christian saint of the name whose feast-day is 3 May.

CLOTHRU: CLOTHRA (klō-ra) f, meaning, perhaps, 'famous'. In story Clothru was daughter of king Eochu Feidlech, sister of Medb queen of Connacht, and mother of the warrior Lugaid Riab nDerg. There was also a virgin saint of the name who is patroness of Inchdoney, Co Cork, and whose feast-day is 1 October. It could be anglicised *Clora*.

CNES: CNEAS (kn'as) f. Meaning literally 'skin' but figuratively, perhaps, 'fair of form, beautiful'. In the legends of the saints, Cnes was mother of St Mac Nisse of Connor.

COBLAITH: COBHLAITH (kov-la) f. Meaning, perhaps, 'sovereignty, victorious sovereignty'. This name was relatively common in the early Irish period and has on occasion been anglicised *Cowley*. It was borne by among others the daughter of Cano, an early Scottish king and hero of an early Irish romance; by the daughter of the powerful Leinster king, Cellach Cualann, who died in 731; and by an abbess of Kildare who died in 916.

COBTHACH: COBHTHACH, COFACH (kov-hach) m, 'victorious'. This name was popular in the early period, particularly in the southern half of Ireland. It was borne by one of the legendary ancestors of the Eóganacht and Dál Cais. Cobthach Cóel Breg ('the Slender of Brega') was one of the early legendary heroes of the Uí Néill and among the historical bearers of the name were Cobthach, king of the Déisi, who died in 632, and Cobthach mac Maíle Dúin, king of west Munster, who died in 833. This name was popular among the O Fallons, O Maddens and other families and was latinised *Coganus*. From it derive the modern surnames (O) Coffey and (O) Cowhig.

COCCÁN (kuk-ān) m. Meaning, perhaps, 'red'. A rare early name.

COCHRANN (kuch-ran) f. Meaning, perhaps, 'red lady'. Cochrann was the daughter of the legendary king of Leinster, Cathaír Már, and mother of Diarmait úa Duibne, the greatest lover in Irish legend.

*COILÍN (kol'-īn') m. This name derives from *Nicholas*, through the French abbreviation *Col*. Originally the name of a saintly bishop of Myrna who flourished about 300 A.D., it became a favourite name in England in the twelfth century whence it was brought into Ireland by the Normans, where it became relatively popular in the middle ages. The usual English and Scottish form is *Colin*.

CÓILÍN (kōl'-īn') m. Supposed to be a modern diminutive form of *Colmán*, now in use only in Connemara.

COLCU: COLGA (kul-ga) m. This name was relatively popular in the early period. Its most famous bearer was St Colcu úa Duinechda, bishop and hermit, who was author of a devotional work called the *Broom of Piety*. He died in 796 and his feast-day is 20 February.

COLLA (ku-la) m. Meaning, perhaps, 'great lord, chief'. The most famous bearers of this name were the three Collas, three brothers who are regarded as the founders of the early kingdom of Oriel and ancestors of many great families including the O Kellys of Connacht, the Maguires, MacMahons (of Ulster), MacDonnells and MacSweeneys. In the middle ages and early modern period the name is found principally among those very families and it survived in Antrim and Omeath down to the late nineteenth century, especially among the MacDonnells. It was occasionally anglicised *Coll*.

COLMÁN (kul-măn) m.   A diminutive of *Columb*, from Latin *columba* 'a dove'. Colmán is the fourteenth most popular male name in early Ireland and there are, according to an early text, some 234 saints of the name. Amongst the most famous of these saints are St Colmán Elo of Lynally, Co Westmeath, whose feast-day is 26 September; St Colmán mac Léníne, patron of the diocese of Cloyne, whose feast-day is 24 November; Colmán mac Duach of the royal race of Connacht, patron of Kilmacduagh, whose feast-day is 2 January; St Colmán of Kilcolman, Co Offaly, 'of the blood of the kings of Munster', whose feast-day is 20 May; St Colmán mac Lúacháin of Lynn, Co Westmeath, whose feast-day is 14 June; and St Colmán of Lismore whose feast-day is 22 January. Another famous saint of the name is St Colmán, the pilgrim-bishop, who wished to traverse Hungary and who was beaten to death at Stockerau. Great devotion sprang up to him in Hungary; his name was borrowed into Hungarian as *Kálmán* and is still a popular Hungarian name. In the forms *Colma*, *Colman* the name was also used sparingly as a female name. Colma was one of the three virginal sisters who were disciples of St Comgall at his monastery of Bangor.

*COLUMB: COLUM, COLAM, CALAM, COLM (kul-am) m and f.   From Latin *columba* 'a dove'. There were some thirty-two saints of the name. The most famous of them was undoubtedly Columbcille (otherwise Columba), of the royal race of the Uí Néill and apostle of Scotland, whose feast-day is 9 June. Another famous bearer of the name was St Columb moccu Chremthannán of Terryglass whose feast-day is 13 November. Columb also occurs as a female name in the early pedigrees. One of the female saints of the name is St Columb, daughter of Búite, whose feast-day is 25 March.

COMGALL: COMHGHALL (kow-al) m.   This name was

reasonably common in the early period and there are some ten saints of the name. The most famous of these is St Comgall of Bangor whose feast-day is 10 May. It could be anglicised as *Cowal*.

COMGÁN: COMHGHÁN (kū-ān) m. This relatively rare name was borne by St Comgán of Killeshin, Co Carlow, whose feast-day is 27 February. It could be anglicised *Cowan*.

COMMÁN: COMÁN (kum-ān) m. This name was relatively popular in the early period especially in the south of Ireland. Of the four or so saints of the name, the best known is St Commán of Roscommon whose feast-day is 26 December.

COMNAT: COMNAIT (kum-nit′) f, the female form of *Commán*. St Comnat was a virgin abbess of Kildare whose feast-day is 1 January.

*CONAING (kun-ing) m. A borrowing from Anglo-Saxon *cynyng* 'a king'. The earliest known bearer of the name was the Scots-Irish prince, Conaing mac Aedáin, who died in 621. The name became quite popular in Ireland in the early middle ages and was favoured by the Uí Néill but it fell into disuse at a later period. There is a St Conaing whose feast-day is 23 September.

CONAIRE (kun-ir′-e) m. This name is common enough as the name of legendary heroes but is rare as a name in the historic period. The most famous bearer of the name was the legendary high-king, Conaire Már, hero of the strange fatalistic early Irish tale, the *Burning of Dá Derga's Hostel*. The name is found occasionally at a later period among the O Clery family.

CONALL (kun-al) m, 'strong as a wolf'. A very old, common Celtic name borne by many of the legendary kings and warriors of Ireland. Among its most famous bearers were Conall Cernach, the great Ulster hero; Conall Corc, legendary founder of the kingship of Cashel; Conall Echlúath ('Steedswift'), traditionally the ancestor of the O Briens and related families; and Conall Gulban, ancestor of the O Donnells, O Gallaghers and other Donegal families, who gave his name to *Tír Chonaill*. Among the saints of the name are St Conall of Clondallon, near Newry, whose feast-day is 2 April and St Conall of Iniskeel, near Glenties, whose feast-day is 22 May.The name continued in use among the O Donnells, O Dohertys, O Cannanains, MacEnealises, O Friels, O Gallaghers and MacAwards down to the end of the nineteenth century. The name could be anglicised *Conall* or *Connell*.

CONAMAIL: CONAMHAIL, CONÚIL (kun-ūl′) m, 'wolf-like'. This name occurs reasonably frequently in the early pedigrees. There is also a St Conamail whose feast-day is 8 October.

CONÁN (kun-ān) m, 'hound, wolf'. There were some six saints of this name, one of them a relative of St Columbcille. Conán mac Mórna is one of the principal characters of the Finn-tales. The name is anglicised *Conan*.

CONCHOBAR: CONCHOBHAR, CONCHÚR (kru-hūr) m. Perhaps, meaning 'wolf-lover, lover of hounds'. Conchobar is one of the most favoured Irish names and is especially popular in the later middle ages and early modern period. One of its most famous bearers is Conchobar mac Nessa, king of Ulster in the days of the Red-Branch. Conchobar mac Taidg, who died in 882, is ancestor of the O Connors of Connacht and Conchobar Redbrow is legendary ancestor of the Leinstermen. The name was much favoured by the O Briens, the O Connors of Kerry and Offaly and many other families. As early as the fifteenth century it was equated with the Latin name *Cornelius* with which it has no connection. It has been anglicised *Cornelius, Nelius, Corney, Curney, Neil, Neelusheen, Conny, Con, Cud, Nahor, Naugher, Nohor*. Perhaps the most acceptable form in English is *Connor*.

CONGAL: CONGHAL (kun-īal) m, 'brave, fierce as a hound (wolf)'. One of the more common early Irish names, it was borne by such important personages as Congal Cáech, king of Ulster in the early seventh century and Congal Cennmagair, high-king of Ireland, who died in 710. It could be anglicised *Connell*.

CONGALACH: CONGHALACH (kun-gal-ach, kun-īl-ach) m, from *Congal*. In the early period this was a popular name with a country-wide distribution. Its most famous bearer was, perhaps, Congalach mac Máel Mithig, high-king who died in 956.

CONLÁED: CONLAODH, CONLAO (kun-lē) m. Apart from being borne by two personages in Irish prehistory, this rare name was borne by St Conláed, a saint of Kildare supposed to be St Brigit's craftsman, whose feast-day is 3 May. The name has been anglicised *Conleth* and *Conley*.

CONMACC: CONMHAC (kun-vok) m, 'wolf-son, hound-son'. In Irish pre-history Conmacc was son of the Ulster warrior Fergus mac Róich and ancestor of all the early peoples called Conmaicne. In the later middle ages, the name occurs among the O Farrells and the O Mores. It was anglicised *Canoc*.

CONMÁEL: CONMHAOL (kun-vēl) m, 'wolf-warrior'. A fairly uncommon early name which occurs among the Air-gialla, Osraige and Déisi.

CONN (kun, kown) m. Perhaps meaning 'wisdom' or 'chief'. It could also be a pet-form of a name in *Cú (Con)*. The most famous bearer of this ancient name was Conn Cétchathach ('of the hundred battles'), legendary ancestor of the kings of Ireland and of many Irish noble families including the O Neills and O Donnells of Ulster and the O Connors, O Rourkes, O Flahertys and O Dowds of Connacht. It was a favourite name among the O Neills, O Donnells, O Rourkes and Mac Brannons and was used in almost all Donegal families until the end of the last century. In modern times, it was anglicised as *Constantine*.

CONNA (kun-a) m and f, a pet-form of *Colmán* (which see). There is also a female St Conna (or Condath), a patroness of the southern Uí Néill, whose feast-day is 3 February.

CONNLA, CONDLA: CONNLA, CÚNLA (kūn-la) m. Meaning, perhaps, 'great lord, great chief'. This name is the same in origin as *Colla* (which see). There is a St Condla, a bishop whose feast-day is 10 May. It was borne by a number of ecclesiastics and remained in use down to the seventeenth century and later. Connla is also the hero of the bawdy modern Irish ballad. The name has been anglicised *Conle* or *Conly*.

CONRÍ (kun-rī) m, 'king of wolves, king of hounds'. A name which occurs occasionally in the earliest pedigrees, it could be anglicised *Conry*.

*CONSTANS m. A borrowing of Latin *constans* 'firm, constant'. It was in use in classical antiquity and was borne, by among others, Constans, son of Constantine the Great. It was in occasional use among clerics in early Christian Ireland but never became popular. A female name *Constance* (from Latin *constantia* 'constancy') is one of the current favourite fancy names in England.

CORBB: CORB (kurb) m. Probably related to the verb *corbbaid* 'defiles'. This name is borne only by legendary persons in early Irish literature. The diminutive forms *Corbbéne* and *Corbbán* occur in the early pedigrees and could be anglicised *Corban*. The well-known name *Cormac* (which see) is probably a compound of *Corbb* and *macc* 'a son'.

CORBBACH: CORBACH (kurb-ach) f, from *Corbb* (which see). A relatively rare female name borne by at least one saint.

CORBBNAT: CORBNAIT (kurb-nit') f, female form of *Corbbán*. It was also a saint's name.

CORCC: CORC (kurk) m. There is a very old word *corc* 'heart' but the early Irish writers believed that *corcc* meant 'red, crimson'. Corcc occurs in the early legendary materials and in the later middle ages almost exclusively in Munster, where it was relatively common. Corcc mac Luigdech is the legendary founder of the kingship of Cashel and ancestor of many kings of Munster. There is also a St Corcc of Kilmore, near Armagh, whose feast-day is 4 April. Corcc was favoured amongst the O Moriartys of Kerry in the twelfth century and was in use among the O Keeffes in the thirteenth and fourteenth centuries. From it derives the modern surname Ó Cuirc (O Quirke), a prominent Munster family.

CORCCAIR: CORCAIR (kurk-ir') f, derived from *Corcc*

(which see). This name was borne by a number of aristocratic Munster ladies in the early middle ages.

CORCCÁN: CORCÁN (kurk-ān) m, a diminutive form of *Corcc* (which see). A relatively uncommon early name borne by at least one saint.

CORCRÁN (kurk-rān) m. Probably from *corcur* 'red, crimson, purple'. Among others, this name was borne by Corcrán Clérech, a famous hermit of Lismore, who died in 1040 and by St Corcrán whose feast-day is 8 October. The name gives the modern surname Ó Corcráin (Corcoran).

CORMACC: CORMAC (kur-mok) m. For derivation, see *Corbb*. Cormac is perhaps the tenth most popular name in early Ireland. Among its legendary bearers are Cormac mac Airt, king of Tara and ancestor of the Uí Néill; Cormac Cas mac Ailella Óluim, legendary ancestor of the O Briens, Mac Namaras and other Dál Cais families; and Cormac Gelta Gáeth, legendary ancestor of the Leinstermen. Among the historical bearers of the name are Cormac mac Ailella, king of Munster, who died in 713; Cormac mac Cuilennáin, king, bishop and scholar, who was slain in 908; and Cormac Mac Carthaig, king of Munster and builder of Cormac's Chapel at Cashel, who was slain in 1138. Among the saints of the name are St Cormac whose feast day is 10 May; St Cormac, bishop of Trim, whose feast-day is 17 February; and St Cormac of Aran whose feast-day is 11 May. According to legend, this last Cormac asked the devil the way to heaven and the devil gave him very good advice. Cormac remained a popular name throughout Ireland at all periods but in the seventeenth century, especially after Charles I became king of England, many Irish families of distinction including the MacCarthys, changed the name to *Charles*.

CORMACCÁN: CORMACÁN (kur-mok-ān) m, a diminutive of *Cormac* (which see). The most distinguished bearer of this name was Cormacán mac Maíl Brigde, one of the chief poets of Ireland who died in 948. From it derives the modern surname Ó Cormacáin (Cormican).

COSRACH (kus-krach) m, 'triumphant, victorious'. This

60

was a relatively common name between the eighth and the tenth centuries. Coscrach, a scribe and hermit, died in 867. It gives rise to the modern surname Ó Coscraigh which has been anglicised as Cosgrave and Cosgrove. *Coscrachán* is a relatively rare diminutive form of *Coscrach*.

COSNUMACH: COSNAMHACH (kus-nŭch) m, 'contentious, valiant'. This name was in use among the O Boyles, O Mulloys, MacClancys and other families. It was anglicised as *Constantine* and *Constance*. The names *Cosnumach* and *Cosnaidhe* are apparently interchangeable.

CRANAT: CRANAIT (kran-it') f. The only bearer of this name known to me is St Cranat, a patron saint of the district about Fermoy, Co Cork, who traditionally flourished in the sixth century. Popular devotion to her continued in that district until the beginning of this century.

CRÉD, CRÉDE: CRÉDH, CRÉIDHE (kr'ē) f. There are a number of famous ladies in Irish literature and history called Créd. According to story, Créd was daughter of the famous Guaire Aidne (king of Connacht), wife of Marcán (king of Uí Maine), and mistress to Cano mac Gartnáin (a Scottish king). In later times, the O Connors of Connacht claimed her as their ancestress. Another Créd was daughter of Cairbre, king of Ciarraige. The warrior Cáel fell in love with her and won her and she died of sorrow when Cáel was slain at the battle of Ventry (*cath Finntrágha*).

CRÍCHÁN: CRECHÁN (kr'īch-ān) m, 'hoarse'. A relatively rare early name from which derive the modern surnames Creaghan, Crehan.

CRIMTHANN: CRIOMTHANN, CRIOFAN (kr'i-fan) m, 'a fox'. Crimthann was one of the most popular names in early Ireland. Crimthann Már mac Fidaig was a legendary king of Ireland and the name was borne by a number of early Munster kings. According to the Finn-ballads, there were ten warriors of the name among the followers of Finn mac Cumaill. There was also a St Crimthann whose feast-day is 23 May and, according to story at least, Crimthann was Columbcille's first name. From this derives the surname

Mac Criomthainn (Mac Crohan), the name of a well known branch of the O Sullivans in Kerry. Among the Kavanaghs it was anglicised *Creon, Crehan, Criffin* and eventually *Griffin*. It was sometimes latinised *Gregorius*.

CRÍNÁN: CRÍONÁN (kr'īn-ān) m, 'old'. A relatively rare name found chiefly in early Munster. Crinán mac Faílbe, king of Corcu Duibne (†1027), was ancestor of the Uí Faílbe (O Falveys).

CRÍNÓC: CRÍONÓG (kr'īn-ōg) f, from *crín* 'old'. A Munster princess called Crínóc died in 1044.

CRÍTÁN: CRÍODÁN (kr'īd-ān) m. This early name was borne by three saints: St Crítán whose feast-day is 17 May; St Crítán, also called Mo-Chrítóc, whose feast-day is 8 October; and St Crítán mac Illadon who dwelt by the banks of the Dodder and whose feast-day is 11 May. From Crítán derives the modern surname O Críodáin (O Creedon).

CRÓCHNAT: CRÓCHNAIT (krōch-nit') f. From *cróch* 'saffron, red'. In the Finn-ballads Cróchnait was the mother of the warriors Diarmait and Oscar.

CRÓEBNAT: CRAOBHNAIT (krēv-nit') f. Derived, perhaps from *cróeb* 'a branch, a garland'. St Cróebnat was a virgin saint whose feast-day is 17 July. *Cróeb* also occurs as a female name and saint's name. There is a male form *Cróebán, Cróebíne*.

CROMMÁN: CROMÁN (krum-ān) m. From *cromm* 'crooked, bent'. A name which may have been especially applied to clerics but which is very rare.

CRÓN (krōn) f, 'saffron-coloured, yellow, swarthy'. This name was borne by some seventeen female saints in early Ireland. *Cróine* appears to be derived from it. There were two well-known saints called Cróine, St Cróine of the southern Uí Néill whose feast-day is 27 January and St Cróine of Tempall Cróine in Tír Conaill whose feast-day is 7 July.

CRÓNÁN (krōn-ān) m. Derived from *crón* 'swarthy, yellow'. Though rare enough as a secular name, Crónán is common among the saints' names. Among the best-known of the name are St Crónán, bishop of Antrim, whose feast-day is 7 January; St Crónán, abbot of Tuaim Gréne (Tomgraney), whose feast-day is 19 October; St Crónán of Roscrea, also called Mo-Chua, whose feast-day is 28 April; and St Crónán of Slieve Phelim whose feast-day is 4 May. In the form *Croney* the name is still traditional among the O Hogans of north Tipperary.

CRÓNSECH: CRÓINSEACH (krōn'-s'ach) f, female form of *Crónán*. Crónsech was the daughter of an early king of Ossory. There is also a St Crónsech whose feast-day is 23 July.

CRUIMMÍNE: CRUIMÍN (krim-īn'). From *cromm* 'crooked, bent'. St Cruimmíne was bishop of Lackan in Westmeath and his feast-day is 28 June. The name could be anglicised *Cremin*.

CRUIMSECH: CRUIMSEACH (krim'-s'ach) f, female form of *Cruimmíne* or *Crommán*. A relatively rare name, there being one saint of the name.

CRUIND: CRUINN (krin') m, 'round'. A relatively rare name, the most famous bearer of which was Cruind ba Druí, an early king of the Ulaid and founder of a royal dynasty. O Rahilly suggested that Cruind was another name for the sun-deity.

CÚ CHAILLE: CÚ CHOILLE (kū chil'e) m, 'wolf or hound of the wood'. A rare early name.

CÚ CHOIGCRÍCHE: CÚ COIGRÍCHE (kū kig'-r'īhe) m, 'hound of the border'. This name was peculiar to the families of O Molloy, Mageoghegan and a few other midland families and to the learned family of O Clery. The name has been anglicised *Peregrine*. The surname Mac Conchoigríche, which derives from it, has been everywhere anglicised *Lestrange*.

CÚ CHONNACHT (kū chun-acht) m, 'hound of the Connacht-men'. This was a favourite name among the Maguires and O Reillys in the later middle ages. It was also in use among the learned family of O Daly. It has been anglicised *Constantine* among the Maguires.

CÚ CHULAINN (kū chul-in′) m. Cú Chulainn is the greatest of all Irish warriors and the hero of the epic tale *Táin Bó Cualgne*. He is matchless in strength, in beauty and in skill at arms, and defended Ulster single-handed against the armies of Connacht.

CÚ DUB: CÚ DHUBH (kū-uv) m, 'black hound'. This name occurs among the Uí Faílbe (O Falveys) of Corcu Duibne in the twelfth and early thirteenth centuries.

CÚ FAIFNE: CÚAIFNE (kū af′-ne) m, 'hound of Faffand' (a district in ancient Offaly). This name is found almost exclusively among the O Connors of Uí Failge (Offaly) in the middle ages.

CÚ LUACHRA (kū luach-ra) m, 'hound of Lúachair' (a district in ancient Kerry). This name is in use among the Uí Chonchobair (O Connors) of Kerry in the twelfth and thirteenth centuries.

CÚ MAIGE: CÚ MHAIGHE, CÚMHAÍ (kū-vī, kū-ī), 'hound of the plain'. This name is relatively rare in the very early period but in the later middle ages it is especially common among the MacMahons, MacCawells, MacCanns, O Flynns, O Kanes, MacLochlainns and MacCloskeys. It was anglicised *Quintin* and *Quinton* among many of these families but it has also been anglicised *Cooey* and *Hughey* and thus confused with *Áed* (which see), which has been anglicised *Hugh* with a diminutive *Hughie* or *Hughey*.

CÚ MARA: CÚ MHARA (kū-var-a) m, 'hound of the sea'. One of the chief bearers of this name was Cú Mara mac Liag, principal poet of Ireland, who died in 1030. The name was favoured by the O Mahoneys and the Meic Conmara (MacNamaras) and from it they derived their surnames. It was anglicised *Cowvarre*.

CÚ MEDA: CÚ MHEADHA, CÚMHEÁ (kū-v′ā) m, 'mead-hound'. This name is found, to my knowledge, only in the family of Meic Conmara (MacNamara). It has been anglicised *Cuvea*.

CÚ ROÍ: CÚ RAOI (kŭ-rī) m.   The meaning of this name
is doubtful and among the explanations which have been
offered are 'hound of the plain' and 'hound of (the god)
Rua'. Cú Roí was a legendary Munster hero. According
to saga, 'Ireland could not contain him for his haughtiness,
renown and rank, overbearing fury, strength and gallantry.'
Despite its pagan associations the name was borne by the
scholarly cleric and learned historian, Cú Roí mac Aildniad
of Inis Cloghran on Lough Ree, who died in 871.

CÚ ULAD: CÚ ULADH, CÚ ULA (kŭ-ul-a) m, 'hound of
the Ulstermen'.   This name is common in the early period
among the families of Ulaid and Airgialla. In the later period
it is found among the Uí Chaíndelbáin (O Kindallons) of
Meath, the O Flynns, MacMahons, O Neills, Maguires, Mac
Ardles and the MacKearneys of Ulster. The last MacKearney
of the name changed it to *James*. It has been variously
anglicised *Cullo*, *Cullowe* and *Cooley* and has been turned
into Latin as *Catholicus*.

CÚACH (kŭach) f.   This name was borne by St Cúach,
a virgin saint of Cell Chúaiche (Kilcock), whose feast-day
is 8 January.

CÚACHNAT: CÚACHNAIT (kŭach-nit') f.   St Cúachnat
was a virgin saint whose feast-day is 13 February.

CÚÁN: CUÁN (kŭän) m, diminutive of *cú* 'hound, wolf'.
The name is the exact equivalent of *Conán* (which see).
The name was relatively common in Munster and Cúán
mac Amalgada was an early king of Munster. Cúán ua
Lóthcháin, who was slain by the men of Teffia in 1024,
was the principal poet of Ireland in his day. There was
also a St Cúán of Wexford who gave his name to Kilquan
and whose feast-day is 10 July. From this name is derived
the surname Ó Cuáin (O Quane, Quain).

CÚANU: CUANA (kŭan-a) m.   This name has been explained as meaning 'distinguished, pleasant' but it could also
be a pet-form derived from a compound name in *cú* 'hound,
wolf'. Its most famous bearer in Irish literature was Cúana
mac Ailchíne, an early warrior and king of the Fermoy

district.

CÚANACHTACH (kūan-acht-ach) m, 'leader of a wolf-pack or of a band of warriors'. A relatively rare early name.

CUILÉN: COILEÁN (kil'-ān) m, 'a whelp', hence, 'a youth, young warrior'. This name was common among Munster peoples especially the Dál Cais. Clann Chuiléin ('the family of Cuilén') was the family name of the MacNamaras and related families. The name was favoured by the Uí Dímmusaig (O Dempseys) in the later middle ages. Cuilén Ua Domnalláin, judge of Offaly, died in 1065. There is also a St Cuilén of Lowhill, Co Offaly, whose feast-day is 22 April. In the form *Colin* it was a favoured name in the House of Argyll (Campbells) but this may be derived from *Coilín* (which see).

CUIMMÍNE: CUIMÍN (kim'-īn') m. From *camm* 'crooked, bent'. This was the name of three distinguished early Irish saints: St Cuimmíne of Dál Cais whose feast-day is 1 June; St Cuimmíne Fata of Clonfert whose feast-day is 12 November; and St Cuimmíne Finn, abbot of Iona, who died in 669 and whose feast-day is 24 February. The name has been anglicised *Cummian*, *Cumin*, and *Comyn*.

CUINCHE (kin-he) f. This rare name was borne by the abbess of Rossmanagher and fosterer of St Ciarán of Seir.

CUINDLES: CUINNLEAS (kin'-l'as) m. A relatively rare early name. Cuindles, abbot of Clonmacnoise, died in 724. From this name derives the modern surname Ó Cuindlis (O Quinlish, Quinlisk).

CUIRITHIR (kir'-i-hir') m. The only bearer of this name known to me is Cuirithir the poet and lover of Líadan. When he came to marry her, she was already a nun. He became a monk and, like Abelard and Heloise, they remained in love.

CUMMAN, CUMMAIN, CUMNE (kum-an) f. This name occurs in legend and in early history. St Cumman was a female saint of the Ards of Ulster whose feast-day is 29 May.

CURCHACH (kurch-ach) f. There were two saints of the

name: St Curchach, patroness of Clonlogher, near Manor-hamilton, whose feast-day is 8 August and St Curchach, patroness of Kilcorkey to the west of Elphin, Co Roscommon, whose feast-day is 21 July.

CURNÁN: (kurn-ān) m. The best-known bearer of this name is St Curnán of Kilcornan, in Kenry, Co Limerick, whose feast-day is 6 January.

DAGÁN: DAGHÁN (dag-án, da-án) m.   Derived from *dag* — 'good'. There were two saints of the name, bishop Dagán, whose feast-day is 12 March and St Dagán of the area about Arklow whose feast-day is 13 September.

DAGAIN: DAGHAIN (dein) f.   Perhaps from *dag* — 'good'. This name was borne by a virgin saint of the Leinstermen.

DAIG: DAIGH (dei) m, 'flame, fire'.   This was a relatively common name in early Ireland. It was borne by a son of Énna Cennselach, legendary ancestor of the MacMurroughs, Kinsellas and other south Leinster families. St Daig mac Cairill is patron of Iniskeen, Co Louth, and his feast-day is 18 August.

DAIGRE: DAIGHRE (dei-r′e) m.   From *daig* 'flame, fire'. In the Finn ballads Daigre was one of the musicians to the Fian. There is also a St Daigre of Meath whose feast-day is 30 September.

DAIMÍNE, DAIMÉNE: DAIMHÍN (dov′-in′) m.   From *dam* 'a deer, an ox'. This name was particularly borne by the legendary heroes of the Airgialla. According to legend, Daimíne Damargait, king of Airgialla, was one of the three kings who went to heaven in the lifetime of St Columbcille. From this name derive the modern surnames Davin, Devin and Devine. It could be anglicised *Davin*.

DÁIRE (dá-r′e) m and f.   From an old root meaning 'fruitful, to make fruitful, fertile'. Dáire is one of the commonest names in Irish legend and mythology and seems to be the name of an early bull-god or god of fertility. In secular sources the name is almost invariably a divine name. In ecclesiastical legend, St Patrick was granted the site of his church at Armagh by a landowner called Dáire. There is a Saint Dáire whose feast-day is 20 December. It occurs rarely as a female name being borne by one virgin Saint Dáire whose feast-day is 8 August. The name occurs occasionally amongst the learned family of Ó Bruaideda (O Brody, O Briody) of Thomond.

DÁIRINE (dā-r′i-n′e) f. Derived, perhaps, from *Dáire* (which see). Dáirine and her sister, Fithir, were two daughters of the legendary king of Tara, Túathal Techtmar. The foster-mother of St Colmán of Daire Mór was also called Dáirine.

DÁLACH (dāl-ach) m, 'one surrounded by companies, one given to frequenting assemblies'. Of the early bearers of the name one may mention Dálach, abbot of Fore, who died in 1011 and Dálach, abbot of Duleek, who died in 820. From this name derives the surname Ó Dálaigh (O Daly), one of the premier learned families of medieval Ireland.

DALBACH: DALBHACH (dol-vach) m. Meaning, perhaps, 'guileful, full of sorcery'. The best-known bearer of this name was St Dalbach of Cúl Collainge (Coole, in eastern Co Cork), who died in 800 and whose feast-day is 23 October. It was in use among the O Byrnes and other Leinster families until the seventeenth century.

DALLÁN (dol-ān) m. From *dall* 'blind'. Among the more famous bearers of this name are Dallán mac More, poet to Cerball, king of Leinster and Dallán Forgaill a famous early poet who composed a lament for Columbcille. There is a St Dallán who gave his name to the parish of Kildallon, near Killeshandra — an area in which the name is in current use in the form *Dallan*.

DAMÁN: DAMHÁN (dav-ān) m, 'little stag, little ox'. Damán Clérech of the royal race of Airgialla (Oriel) is a northern saint whose feast-day is 12 February. Áed Damán was an early king of west Munster who died in 633. The name could be anglicised *Davin* or *Davan*.

DAMNAT: DAMHNAIT (dav-nit′) f, 'fawn, little deer'. Damnat, wife of Áed Bennán, king of Munster, is ancestress of the O Moriartys, O Cahills, O Flynns, O Carrolls and other Kerry families. There is also a St Damnat associated with Slieve Beagh and Tedavnet, Co Monaghan, whose feast-day is 13 May. On occasion, she has been identified with a celebrated Irish virgin, called *Dymphna* or *Dympna*, who was martyred in Gheel in Belgium and who is venerated as a patroness of the insane. Damnat has been anglicised as *Devnet*, *Davnit*, *Downet*, *Dymphna* and *Dympna*.

*DANIÉL m. This biblical name was borrowed by a number of early Irish clerics such as Daniél abbot of Roscrea (†761) and Daniél abbot of Arbrackan (†736). It never became popular in Ireland and, of course, has no connection with the Celtic name *Domnall* (which see), with which it has frequently been equated.

DANU: DANA f. This is a later learned form of the early name *Anu* (which see).

DATHAL (do-hal) m. Perhaps from *daith* 'swift, nimble'. An early name which occurs amongst the people of Fermoy. It could be anglicised *Dahal*.

DAUI, DAU, DUÍ, DUACH (dow-ī, dow, duach) m. In the case of this name a number of separate names may have fallen together and become confused. Among its famous bearers are Daui Iarlaithe, legendary ancestor of the Eóganacht of Killarney; Duí Galach, ancestor of the O Connor kings of Connacht, and a number of early founders of dynasties. The name seems to have fallen largely into disuse by the seventh century.

*DAUÍD: DAIBHEAD m. A borrowing of the biblical name *David* which was introduced to Ireland by the Anglo-Normans and which became a common name amongst the Burkes and among aristocratic Munster families in the later middle ages. The pet-forms *Dabacc*, *Dabag* and *Dabhag* were common in the later middle ages. It gives the modern surnames Davitt and MacDevitt. The most common Irish form is now *Dáibhí*.

DECLÁN: DEAGLÁN (d'eg-lān) m. St Declán, whose
feast-day is 24 July, is the founder of the monastery of
Ardmore, Co Waterford, and, as patron of the Déisi, bears
the title 'Patrick of Déisi'. The name has been anglicised
Declan and has recently achieved a measure of popularity.

DELBNAT: DEALBHNAIT (d'alv-nit') f. Derived, perhaps,
from *delb* 'shape'. Delbnat is patroness of Abbeylara, Co
Longford.

DELLA: DEALLA (d'al-a) f. Della was one of the women
who came to Ireland in the legendary pre-Deluge invasion led
by queen Cessair.

DEMMÁN: DEAMÁN (d'am-ān) m. An early pet-form
of the well-known name Diarmait. Its most famous bearer
was Demmán mac Cairill (†572), an early king of Ulster.
It could be anglicised *Deman*.

DER ÁINE, DARÁINE (dor-ān'e) f, 'daughter of (the goddess)
Áine'. A rare early name.

DER BILE, DAR BILE: DEIRBHILE (d'er'-v'il'-e) f.
St Der Bile was a saint of Connacht whose feast-day is 26
October. It could be anglicised *Dervila* or *Dervla*.

DERBÁIL, DER BFÁIL: DEARBHÁIL (d'ar-vāl') f. Meaning, perhaps, 'daughter of Fál (a legendary name for Ireland)';
see *Bé Fáil*. Derbáil was a popular name in medieval Ireland.
Among its bearers were Derbáil, grand-daughter of the high-
king, Aed Oirnide, and wife of Flannacán mac Cellaig, king
of Brega, who died in 931; Derbáil daughter of the high-king
Congalach mac Máel Mithig; and Derbáil, daughter of the king
of Connacht, who died in 1010. Derbáil was a popular name
among the MacDermotts of Connacht in the later middle
ages. It could be anglicised *Derval* or *Dervilia*.

DERBILED, DAR FILED: DEIRBHILE, DAIRILE (d'er'-
v'il'e, dar'-il'e) f, 'daughter of a poet'. There are at least
two saints of the name, St Derbiled of Erris, Co Mayo,
and St Derbiled of the royal race of Connacht whose feast-
day is 3 August. It could be anglicised *Dervila*.

DERDRIU: DEIRDRE (d'er'-dr'e) f. The meaning of this

name is much in doubt. It could be a pet-form of a name in *der*—or it could be a very old name meaning 'she who murmurs, chatters'. In Irish legend Derdriu is a tragic heroine. She was the daughter of Feidlimid of the Tuatha Dé Danann, harper and story-teller to Conchobar, king of Ulster. Her elopement with Noíse, son of Uisliu, led to her tragic death. The popularity of Derdriu as a girl's name dates from the Celtic revival and in particular from Yeats' *Deirdre* (1907) and Synge's *Deirdre of the Sorrows* (1910).

DER ERCA, DAR ERCA: DAREARCA (dor-ark-a) f. Meaning, perhaps, 'daughter of Erc'. There are some four female saints of this name, the best known being St Darerca whose feast-day is 15 January and the virgin Darerca whose feast-day is 9 September. Darerca was also the name of the mother of St Mel of Longford and, in legend, she is sister of St Patrick and mother of seventeen bishops. Darerca was also the name of the mother of St Ciarán of Clonmacnoise.

DER FINN, DAR FINN: DELRBHINN, DAIRINN (d'er'-v'in, dar'-in') f. Meaning, perhaps, 'daughter of Finn'. Der Finn Bélihota was another name for Eithne, mother of St Columbcille. The name could be anglicised *Dervin* or *Derinn*.

DER BFORGAILL: DEARBHORGAILL (d'ar-vor-gil') f, 'daughter of Forgall' (a god)'. Among the better known bearers of the name are Derbforgaill daughter of the king of Lochlainn and wife of Lugaid Riab nDerg who died of sorrow after her death and Derbforgaill wife of Tigernán Ó Ruairc, king of Breifne, who eloped with Dermot Mac Murrough, king of Leinster, and who later repented and founded the Nuns' Church at Clonmacnoise. The name has been anglicised *Dervorgilla*.

DER LUGA, DAR LUGA: DEARLOGHA, DEARLÚ (d' arlŭ) f, 'daughter of (the god) Lug'. Der Luga is a virgin saint whose feast-day is 10 February.

DER LUGACH, DER LUGDACH: DEARLUACH (d'ar-lŭach) f, 'daughter of Lugaid'. Der Lugach was abbess of

Kildare in succession to St Brigit. She left Ireland and, according to tradition, founded the church of Abernethy in Scotland.

DER ÓMA, DAR ÓMA (dar-ōv-a) f, 'daughter of (the god) Ogmios'. In Irish legend Dar Óma is daughter of Conchobar mac Nessa, king of Ulster. The name could be anglicised *Darova*.

DESMUMHNACH (d'as-ūn-ach) m, 'man from Desmond'. This name occurs only in one late medieval text as the ancestor of the Cork family Ó Deasmhumhnaigh (Desmond). I find no early authority for the modern irregular Irish *Deasún*. The English *Desmond* is probably borrowed directly from the place-name, Desmond, and the modern Irish *Deasún* seems to be a translation of it. From Ireland it passed to England where it has achieved a measure of popularity.

DIANACH (d'īan-ach) m, from *dian* 'swift'. Dianach of Kilbarron, near the Erne, was a saintly bishop whose feast-day is 16 January.

DIANAIM: DIANAIMH (d'īan-iv) f, 'flawless'. This name occurred amongst the aristocratic ladies of Leinster in the tenth and eleventh centuries.

DIARMAIT: DIARMAID (d'īar-mit') m. Despite the many suggestions that have been made, we can attach no definite meaning to this old name which is one of the twenty or so most popular names in early Ireland. Among its legendary bearers was Diarmait úa Duibne of the Finn-tales, the greatest lover in Irish literature and hero of the tale, 'The Pursuit of Diarmait and Gráinne'. Perhaps the best-known of its historical bearers were Diarmait mac Cerbaill (†565), high-king and probably the last great pagan monarch in Ireland; Diarmait Rúanaid, high-king, who died in 665; and Diarmait Mac Murrough, king of Leinster, who invited the Anglo-Normans to Ireland. Among the saints of the name are Diarmait mac Mechair patron saint of Magheraboy, Co Fermanagh, whose feast-day is 16 January; St Diarmait of Inis Clothrann, on Loch Ree, whose feast-day is 10 January; and St Diarmait úa Áeda Róin of the royal race of Ulster, founder of Castledermot, whose feast-day is 21 June. The name was particularly common among the MacCarthys, O Briens, O Connors, MacDermotts and other Irish families in the medieval and modern period. It has been very incorrectly anglicised as *Jeremy, Jeremiah, Jerh, Miah, Jerome, Jarmy, Jerry*, and *Darby*. More recently, it has been anglicised *Dermot* and *Derry*.

DÍCHÚ: DÍOCHÚ (d'í-chū) m, a pet-form of *Dícuill* (which see). The name seems to have been found chiefly in the north of Ireland. There is a St Díchú whose feast-day is 17 November.

DICNAT: DIGNAIT (d'ig-nit') f. This rare name was borne by the sister of St Fintan of Clonenagh.

DÍCUILL (d'í-kil') m. This name is relatively common in the early period but it falls into disuse in the later middle ages. There are pet-forms *Díchú* and *Mo-Díchú*. There were three saints of the name: St Dícuill whose feast-day is 1 May, St Dícuill whose feast-day is 17 November and St Dícuill of Lough Erne whose feast-day is 28 February. The most famous bearer of the name was Dícuill the Geographer, an Irish scholar at the Carolingian court in the early ninth century, who wrote works on astronomy, geography and metrics.

DÍGDE, DÍGE: DÍGHE, DÍ (d'í) f. This is an early mythological name for the territorial goddess of Munster. It was also the name of the sister of St Munnu.

DÍGLACH: DÍOLACH (d'íl-ach) m, 'avenger, champion'. This rare early name was borne by a cleric of Durrow, who died in 764.

DÍMMAE, DÍMMA: DÍOMA (d'īm-a) m, a pet-form of *Diarmait* (which see). This was a common name in the early period but it fell into disuse in the later middle ages. Dímma mac Rónáin was an early king of Dál Cais. Among the saints of the name the most notable are Dímma mac Cais whose feast-day is 12 May and Dímma Dub, bishop of Connor, whose feast-day is 6 January.

DÍMMÁN: DÍOMÁN (d'īm-ān) m, diminutive of *Dímmae*

74

(which see). Its best-known bearer was St Dímmán of Iniskeen, Co Louth, whose feast-day is 10 January.

DÍNERTACH: DÍNEARTACH (d'í-n'art-ach) m. Meaning, perhaps, 'of great strength'. This name was largely confined to Munster in the early period Dínertach mac Guaire, king of Uí Fidgeinte (Limerick), was slain in battle in 649. There is a St Dínertach whose feast-day is 9 October.

DÍMMASACH: DÍOMASACH (d'ĭm-as-ach) m, 'proud, arrogant'. This name was relatively common in the earlier period but later fell into disuse. From it derives the surname O Díomasaigh (O Dempsey).

DOIREND, DAIRENN: DOIREANN (dar'-an) f. Perhaps, identical with *Der Finn* (above). In Irish mythology Doirend is daughter of the fairy-king, Midir. Another Doirend is daughter of Bodh Derg, son of the Dagda ('good god'). She came to woo Finn and gave him a magic potion. The name also occurs in the historic period and one Doirend was mother of Gilla Pátraic, an eleventh-century king of Ossory. Doirend has been wrongly anglicised as *Dorothy* and *Dolly*; *Dorren* is a more acceptable form in English.

DOMNALL: DOMHNALL, DÓNAL (dōn-al) m, 'world-mighty'. This is the ninth most popular name in early Ireland. It was the name of five high-kings including Domnall Ilchelgach ('of the many treacheries'), who died in 566 and was ancestor of the O Neills and Mac Loughlins. There is also a St Domnall whose feast-day is 26 April. In the seventeenth century, Domnall was used as the name for an Irish catholic as *Teague* or *Mick* is in modern English. Since the seventeenth century Domnall has everywhere been equated with the biblical *Daniel*, a name with which it has no connection. In modern slang, *Donie*, a derivative of Domnall, is used to denote the rustic Corkman. In Scotland, Domnall has generally been anglicised *Donald*.

DONN (dun, down) m. This name may mean either 'dun, brown' or 'king, lord'. In Irish mythology Donn is the god of the dead. Tech Duinn ('Donn's house') is the otherworld. Donn was popularly believed to reside in the sandhills of

Dough More, near Doonbeg, Co Clare. In the later medieval period, Donn was a popular name among the Maguires and the O Kennedys and was latinised *Brondus*. It was in use in Derry until the nineteenth century but is now obsolete. From it derives the surname Ó Duinn (O Dunne).

DONNÁN (dun-ān) m, a diminutive of *Donn* (which see). There were four saints of the name, the best-known being St Donnán of Eigg, who was martyred by sea-robbers and whose feast-day is 17 April and St Donnán of Lough Ree, who was reputed to be a brother of St Senán and whose feast-day is 7 January.

DONNCHAD: DONNCHADH, DONNCHA (dun-a-cha) m. From *Donn* meaning 'dun, brown', or 'king, lord'. Donnchad is one of the more common Irish names especially in the later middle ages. It was borne by Donnchad Donn, high-king, who died in 944 and by Donnchad, son of Brian Boru King of Munster, who died in Rome in 1064. It was very common in most Irish families but it has been anglicised as *Dionysius*, *Denis* and *Dinis*, names with which it has no connection. It was also anglicised more acceptably as *Donough*, *Donagh* and in this form it retained its popularity among the O Briens down to modern times. In the north it has, on occasion, been anglicised as *Donaghy*. In medieval times *Donat* and *Donatus*, from Latin *donatus* 'given', were used as equivalents of Donnchad. *Duncan* is the Scottish equivalent.

DONNUCÁN: DONNAGÁN (dun-ag-ān) m, diminutive of *Donn* (which see). From this name derive the surnames O Donegan, Dunnigan and Dongan. The name could be anglicised *Donegan*.

DONNCUAN (dun-kūan, down-kūan) m, 'Donn of the hound-packs'. This name occurs principally in Leinster and Munster in the early period. Donncuan was brother of Brian Boru. It was a favourite name among the Uí Thúathail (O Tooles) and Uí Faílbe (O Falveys) and occurs occasionally among the Dál Cais.

DONNGAL: DONNGHAL (dun-gal, dun-īal) m. Meaning perhaps 'of princely or kingly valour'. One of the more common names in early medieval Ireland. From it derives the modern surname Ó Donnghaile (O Donnelly). The derivative form *Donngalach* also occurs.

DONN SLÉBE: DOINNLÉ (dun-lē-v'e or din'-l'ē) m. Meaning either 'the brown one of the mountain' or the 'lord of the mountain'. This name occurs among the early families of Offaly and south Leinster, among the Uí Gadra (O Garas), and among the Mac Kennas and the people of eastern Ulster where it gave rise to the surname Mac Duinn Slébe (Mac Donleavy), a famous medical family in medieval Ireland.

DONNDUBÁN, DONNUBÁN: DONNABHÁN (dun-av-ān) m, 'dark brown swarthy person'. This name occurs principally in Munster where it is borne by a number of ninth- and tenth-century princes. From it derives the modern surname Ó Donnabháin (O Donovan). It could be anglicised *Donovan*.

DRAIGEN: DRAIGHEAN (drein) f. The word *draigen* means 'blackthorn', which may or may not be connected with this name. In Irish legend Draigen was wife of Mug Nuadat, legendary ancestor of the kings of Munster.

DUARCÁN (dūar-kān) m. Perhaps from *duairc* 'sad, melancholy'. This name occurs among the Meic Thigernáin (Mac Kiernans), Meic In Maigistir (Mac Mastersons) and Uí Egra (O Haras) in the later middle ages. From it derives the surname Ó Duarcáin (Durkan, Dorcan). It could be anglicised *Durkan* or *Dorcan*.

DUAIBSECH: DUAIBSEACH (dūav'-s'ach) f, 'sad, sorrowful, melancholy'. Duaibsech was daughter of Duí Tenga Uma, legendary king of Connacht, and wife of Muirchertach mac Erca, an early high-king.

DUBACÁN: DUBHAGÁN (dū-gān) m. From *dub* 'dark, black' and meaning 'little dark lad'. This name is principally confined to the south of Ireland where it gave rise to the surname Ó Dubhagáin (O Duggan). It could be anglicised as *Duggan* or *Doogan*.

DUBALTACH: DUBHALTACH, DUALTACH (dūal-tach)

m. Meaning, perhaps, 'black jointed, dark-limbed'. This name was particularly common in the later medieval period among the Uí Dochartaig (O Dohertys), Meic Lochlainn (Mac Loughlins) and Uí Gallchobair (O Gallaghers). Perhaps the best-known bearer of the name is Dubaltach Mac Fir Bisigh, the seventeenth-century historian and genealogist and the last great scholar of the old order. This name has generally been anglicised *Dudley* but it became *Dolty* in Donegal while the spoken form in Connemara is *Didley*. It could more properly be anglicised as *Dualtagh* or *Duald*.

DUBÁN: DUBHÁN (duv-án, dū-án) m, 'dark(-haired) person'. In the early pedigrees this name is common enough among the Ciarraige and other Munster peoples. St Dubán was a saintly priest of Hook Point, Co Wexford, whose feast-day is 11 February. In Munster, it gave the surname O Dubáin (O Dwane, Kidney).

DUBCENN, DUBGENN: DUIBHGENN, DUÍGEANN (dī-g'an) m, 'black-haired person'. This name is found among the Dál Cais and the Ossraige but it also occurs in the later middle ages among the O Clerys. It could be anglicised *Deegin* or *Deegan*.

DUBCHOBLAIG: DUBHCHOBHLAIGH (dū-chol-í) f. This name was popular especially in the later middle ages. Dub-choblaig, daughter of the king of Connacht, was wife of Brian Boru and died in 1009. The name was relatively common among the MacDermotts in the thirteenth and fourteenth centuries.

DUBDAE: DUBHDA (dū-da) m. From *dub* 'dark, black'. Dubdae of the Uí Fiachrach is ancestor of the Uí Dubdai (O Dowds, Dodds). There is a St Dubdae whose feast-day is 15 February. The name could be anglicised *Dowd*.

DUB DÁ LETHE (duv-dá-l'e-he) m. This early name was common enough in the south but it also occurs among the hereditary abbots of Armagh. It has been anglicised *Dudley*.

DUB ESSA: DUBH EASA, DUIBHEASA (div'-as-a) f, 'dark (lady) of the waterfall'. Dub Essa was daughter of Amlaíb Ó Donnchadha (O Donoghue) who founded the fortunes of the O Donoghues of Killarney. It was a relatively common name in the thirteenth and fourteenth centuries. It could be anglicised *Devasse*.

DUBGALL: DUBHGHALL (dū-gal) m, 'dark stranger', one of the Irish names for the Vikings. This name occurs only in the north of Ireland and is especially common among the MacSweeneys and O Boyles in the later middle ages. It has been anglicised as *Dougal* and *Dugald*. From it derive the surnames Mac Dubhghaill (MacDowell) and Ó Dubhghaill (O Doyle).

DUBGILLA: DUIBHGHIOLLA (duv'-'il-a) m and f, 'dark lad (lass)'. This relatively uncommon name was borne by a king of Munster and by the wife of Dúnlang, a Leinster prince who died in 911.

DUB LEMNA: DUIBHLEAMHNA (div'l'ow-na) f, 'dark (lady) of Lemain'. Dublemna was daughter of Tigernán, king of Breifne, and wife of the high-king, Donnchad mac Flaind. She died in 943.

DUBTHACH: DUBHTHACH, DUFACH (du-fach) m and f. From *dub* 'dark, black'. Dubthach is one of the commoner early names. Dubthach Dóel Ulad was one of the heroes of the Ulster sagas while Dubthach Lánfhile was one of the legendary early poets. There is a St Dubthach of Tír Chonaill whose feast-day is 5 February, while legend has it that the father of St Brigit was called Dubthach. It occurs rarely as a female name, the principal bearer being Dubthach, daughter of the Ulster hero Eógan mac Durthacht. From it derives the modern surname Ó Dubhthaigh (O Duffy).

DUINNCHAID: DUINNEACHA (din'-ach-a) m. This name is particularly common among the early Munstermen and Leinstermen and gives the modern surname Ó Duinneacha (O Dennehy).

DÚINSECH: DÚINSEACH (dūn'-s'ach) f. This is probably a female form of *Dúnán*, itself a pet-form of a longer name beginning in *dún-* 'a fortress'. It is possible also that another name, *Duinnsech* 'brown-haired girl' is confused with it. There are two saints of the name, St Dúinsech of Ulster whose feast-day is 12 December and St Dúinsech of Carlingford Lough whose feast-day is 5 August. There was a Dúinsech who was daughter of Duí Tenga Uma ('Brazen tongue'), a legendary king of Connacht.

DUINNÍN (din'-ín') m, a diminutive of *Donn* (which see). This name occurs on occasion among the Uí Maíl Chonaire (O Mulconry, Conry) learned family. From it derives the Munster surname Ó Duinnín (Dineen).

DÚNACÁN: DÚNAGÁN (dūn-ag-ān) m. This is a diminutive derived from some longer name beginning in *dún-* 'a fortress'. It is relatively rare.

DÚNADACH: DÚNADHACH (dūn-āch) m, 'one who leads on campaigns'. This is a relatively common name in the early pedigrees and gives the modern surname Ó Dúnadhaigh (O Downey).

DÚNÁN (dūn-ān) m. This is a diminutive derived from a longer name in *dún-* 'a fortress'. It fell into disuse at an early period but from it derives the surname Ó Dúnáin (O Doonan). It could be anglicised *Dunan*.

DÚNCHAD: DÚNCHADH (dūn-cha) m. From *dún* 'a fortress' and *cath* 'a battle'. This name is very common in the early pedigrees and widely distributed throughout Ireland. Later, it became hopelessly confused with *Donnchad* (which see) and was replaced by it. Among the bearers of the name are St Dúnchad, abbot of Iona, whose feast-day is 25 May and Dúnchad, scholar, bishop and chief poet of Ossory, who died in 973.

DÚNCHÁN (dūn-chān) m. A diminutive form of *Dúnchad* which could be anglicised *Duncan*.

DÚNGAL: DÚNGHAL (dūn-gal, dūn-īal) m. From *dún* 'a fortress'. Dúngal is one of the most popular names in early medieval Ireland.

DÚNLAITH (dūn-la) f. Perhaps 'lady of the *dún* (fortress)'. In the saga Dúnlaith is the daughter for the Connacht warrior, Regamon. The name was relatively popular in the early middle ages. It was borne by the wife of the high-king Niall Frassach

80

(†778) and by the daughters of the high-king Flaithbertach mac Loingsig (†765) and Máel Mithig, king of Brega (†942). It could be anglicised *Dunla*.

DÚNLANG (dūn-lang) m.   This name is practically confined to Leinster and Munster in the early pedigrees. Among its bearers were Dúnlang (†988) a Munster king who is ancestor of the O Donoghues and Dúnlang úa Cathail, abbot of Glendalough, who died in 1153. An early Leinster king of the name was ancestor of the O Tooles, O Byrnes and other north Leinster families. From it derives the surname Ó Dúnlaing (O Dowling). In the seventeenth-century manuscripts one finds the form *Dubhlang*. It was anglicised *Dowling* and, later, *Dudley*. It was very common among the Kavanaghs.

ÉBER: ÉIBHEAR (ēv'-ar) m. In the early documents this name is borne by legendary and pseudo-historical personages such as Éber, son of Míl, leader of the Goidelic conquest of Ireland. However, it occurs among the later medieval O Neills and MacMahons and, in the form *Éibhir*, it survived in Derry and Oriel down to the end of the nineteenth century in the families of Magennis and O Lafferty. It has been anglicised *Heber*, *Harry* and *Ivor*.

ÉBLIU, ÉBLENN: ÉIBHLEANN (ēv'-l'an) f. Derived, it is said, from Old Irish *oíph* 'sheen, beauty, radiance' and believed by O Rahilly to be another name for the old Irish sun-goddess. In Irish legend, Ébliu is a supernatural lady who gave her name to the mountains to the south of Nenagh. The name could be anglicised *Evle* or *Evlin*.

ÉCERTACH: ÉIGEARTACH (ēg'-art-ach) m, 'wrong-doer, unjust person'. This early name occurs especially among the Eóganacht of Munster. From it derives the surname Ó hÉigeartaigh (O Hegarty).

ECHDAE: EACHDHA, EACHA (ach-a) m. This has been explained both as 'horse-god' and 'horse-like'. In Irish mythology Echdae was the husband of the goddess Áine.

*ECHDONN: EACHDHONN, EACHANN (ach-an) m. This name has wrongly been explained as derived from Irish *ech* 'a steed' and *donn* 'lord'. In fact, it is a borrowing of the Old Norse name *Hakon*, modern *Haakon*, meaning 'useful, handy'. That name was already borrowed into Irish at an earlier period in the form *Ágonn*. Echdonn has generally been anglicised *Hector* and is still in use in Scotland. Haakon has been corrupted to *Hercules* in the Shetlands.

ECHEN (ech-en) m. Derived from *ech* 'a steed'. This very early name was once common but it fell into disuse in the later period.

ECHMARCACH: EACHMHARCACH (ach-var-kach) m, 'horse-rider'. This was a favourite name among the Mac Brennans of north Connacht but it also occurs in other families. It was anglicised as *Averkagh* in the seventeenth century.

ECHMHÍLIDH (ach-víl-e) m, 'horse-soldier'. This name was very common among the Magennises and MacCartans from the fifteenth to the seventeenth centuries. It was anglicised *Augholy* and latinised *Eugenius*.

ECHNA, ECHNACH: EACHNA (ach-na) f. Probably derived from *ech* 'a steed'. In the Finn-tales Echna was daughter of the king of Connacht. Caílte encountered her as she was playing chess and drinking mead with nine other ladies. According to the story, she was very beautiful and one of the cleverest women in the world.

ECHRAD: EACHRADH, EACHRA (ach-ra) f. Probably derived from *ech* 'a steed'. Echrad was daughter of a tenth-century king of Connacht and was noted for the beauty of her complexion.

ECHRÍ: EICHRÍ (ech'-rí) m, 'lord of steeds'. This is a very old and rare Irish name which occurs also in Gaulish.

ÉCHTACH: ÉACHTACH (ēcht-ach) m and f, 'full of prowess'. In the Finn-tales this name is borne by a son of Oisín and by a daughter of Diarmait and Gráinne, the great lovers in Irish story.

ÉCHTGAL: ÉACHTGHAL (ēcht-gal, ēcht-íal) m, 'capable of prowess, of great exploits'. This early name is common enough in Munster but it is rare elsewhere.

ECHTHIGERN: EACHTHIGHEARN, EACHIARN (ach-íarn),

'lord of steeds'. This was a relatively common name borne, among others, by a brother of Brian Boru and by the father of Flann Mainistrech, a famous early Irish scholar. It could be anglicised *Ahiarn* or *Aherne*. From it derives the modern surname Aherne.

*EIBHLÍN (ei-l'ĭn', ev-'l'ĭn') f. This name was brought to Ireland by the Normans in the forms *Avelina* and *Emeline*. It comes utlimately from Old German and is identical with the English names *Evelina* and *Evelyn*. It was the name of many aristocratic ladies in Norman Ireland—the wife of Walter de Burgo, Earl of Ulster (1271), and the daughter of the Red Earl of Ulster amongst others. It passed to Gaelic Ireland as *Aibhilín* and *Eibhlín*. Aibhilín was the name of a daughter of MacCarthy More in the sixteenth century. As *Eibhlín* the name achieved great popularity. Eibhlín Dubh Ní Chonaill (of the O Connells of Derrynane) composed the greatest of all laments in Irish, *Caoineadh Airt Uí Laoghaire*, on the death of her husband. The name has been re-translated as *Eileen*, *Eily*, *Aileen*, *Eveleen*, *Nellie*, *Nell*, *Helen*, *Ellen*, *Ellie* and *Ella*.

ÉICNECH: ÉIGNEACH (ēg'-n'ach) m. Perhaps from *écen* 'force'. This name is practically confined to the north. There is a St Éicnech whose feast-day is 24 April.

ÉICNECHÁN: ÉIGNEACHÁN (ēg-n'ach-ān) m, diminutive of *Éicnech* (which see). This was a favourite name among the O Donnells especially in the fifteenth and sixteenth centuries. It also occurs among the O Dohertys and other Donegal families and, in the sixteenth century, among the O Kellys. It has been anglicised as *Ignatius*, *Aeneas*, *Eneas* and *Neas*.

ÉLE: ÉILE (ēl'-e) f. In Irish legend Éile was daughter of Eochu Feidlech and sister of the formidable queen of Connacht, Medb.

EISTEN (est'en) f. In the legends of the saints Eisten was the mother of St Faílbe of Westmeath.

EITHNE (eh-n'e) m and f. Eithne is one of the most popular of all early female names. Eithne was mother of the god Lug and of the legendary king Tuathal Techtmar. The wife of Conn Cétchathach ('of the hundred battles') was called Eithne and Eithne Tháebfota ('of the long side') was wife of Cormac mac Airt, legendary king of Tara. One of Cúchulainn's wives was also called Eithne. The name is equally important in ecclesiastical legend. There are nine saints of the name. It is told of St Eithne and her sister Sodelb, both of whom lived near Swords, that Christ used to come to them in the form of a baby and lie in their arms and it was He who baptised them and taught them the faith. Another Eithne was wife of Óengus king of Munster, and mother of St Náile patron of Cell Náile (Kinnawley), Co Fermanagh. The mothers of St M'Áedóc of Ferns and of St Columbcille were also called Eithne. St Eithne, whose feast-day is 6 July, is patroness of Tullow, Co Carlow. The name is also borne by a number of early queens. Eithne, daughter of Bresal of Brega, who died in 768 is known in the annals as 'queen of the kings of Tara'. Eithne, daughter of Domnall Mide the high-king was wife of Bran, king of Leinster, and died in 795. The wife of Congalach mac Máele Mithig, high-king (†953), was also called Eithne. This name has been anglicised *Anne*, *Annie* and *Ena*. In the very early genealogies, Eithne occurs very rarely as a man's name.

*ELÁIR m.   This is a borrowing of the Latin name *Hilarius* 'cheerful'. It was confined to ecclesiastics and the best-known bearer is the hermit St Eláir of Monahincha who died in 807 and whose feast-day is 7 September.

ELATHA: EALADHA (al-a-ha) m, 'art, craft'.   In Irish mythology Elatha is father of the mythical Bress.

ÉLÓDACH: ÉLÁTHACH (ēl-ō-hach) m, 'fugitive, escapee'. This name was relatively common in the earlier period and was borne by one of the ancestors of the O Donoghues.

EILTÍNE, AILTÍNE: EILTÍN (elt'-īn') m.   From *elit* meaning 'a hind' or 'a lively nimble person'. The best-known bearer of the name is St Eiltíne, of the royal race of the Corcu Loígde and patron of Kinsale, whose feast-day is 11 December. He is also known as Mo-Elteóg, a name which is now corrupted to *Multose*. Eiltíne could be anglicised as

Eltin.

*ÉMANN: ÉAMONN m. Émann is a borrowing of the English name Edmond or Edmund, from *ead* 'rich' and *mund* 'protection'. This name was brought into Ireland by the Anglo-Normans where it became popular in the later middle ages. In the seventeenth century Émann was used as a common name for rapparees, hence the expression *maide Éamuinn* (a door-bar to keep rapparees and robbers out.)

EMER (em-er) f. Emer was the beloved of Cúchulainn. According to an early tale she alone of the women of Ireland was wooed by Cúchulainn 'for she had the six gifts: the gift of beauty, the gift of voice, the gift of sweet speech, the gift of needlework, the gift of wisdom and the gift of chastity'.

ÉMÍNE: ÉIMHÍN (ēv'-īn') m. Perhaps from *éim* 'prompt, ready'. This name is found usually in Leinster and Munster. The best-known bearer of the name is St Émíne, bishop and founder of Monasterevan, whose feast-day is 22 November. The name could be anglicised *Evin* or *Evan*.

EMNAT: EAMHNAT (av-nat or av-nit') f. Emnat was mother of St Moling patron of St Mullins. It could be anglicised *Evnat* or *Avnat*.

ÉNÁN (ēn-án) m. According to an early text there are nine saints of this name. The better known are St Énán of Eigg whose feast-day is 29 April and St Énán of the Gorey district whose feast-day is 30 January. The name is anglicised *Enan*.

ÉNNAE: ÉANNA (ē-na) m. The monk who wrote the life of St Énnae of Aran, whose feast-day is 21 March, thought the name meant 'bird-like'. Énnae was also a popular secular name borne by a number of ancient heroes. Énnae Airgthech was a legendary king of Munster. Énna Bóguine was an early king of Connacht and, in Irish prehistory, Énna Cennselach is the ancestor of the kings of south Leinster and of the families of MacMurrough, Kavanagh and Kinsella. This name has been anglicised *Enda*.

EOCHAID, ECHUID: EOCHAIDH, EOCHAÍ (och-í) m.

Meaning, perhaps, 'horse rider', 'fighter on horseback' or some such. *Eochu* (which see) is regarded as a pet-form of Eochaid. Together with Eochu it is the second most popular name in early Irish society. Among the famous legendary bearers of the name are Eochaid Airem, lover of the beautiful and divine Étaín; Eochaid Ballderg, legendary ancestor of the Dál Cais; and Eochaid Mugmedón ('lord of slaves'), an early Irish king and possibly one of those who carried out raids on Roman Britain. Among the saints of the name are St Eochaid, bishop and abbot of Tallaght, whose feast-day is 28 January and St Eochaid, abbot of Lismore, whose feast-day is 17 April. Eochaid Ó hEódhusa (O Hussey) was one of the more distinguished of the later bardic poets. The name has been anglicised *Oghie*, *Oho*, and *Oghe*. The late nineteenth-century northern name *Ataigh* has been regarded as a diminutive of Eochaid and has been translated as *Arthur* in northern Antrim.

EOCHU: EOCHO (och-o) m.   A pet-form of Eochaid with which it is hopelessly confused in the manuscripts. Among the bearers of this name are Eochu Badamna, legendary ancestor of Uí Etersceoil (O Driscolls); Eochu mac Tairdelbaig, ancestor of the Dál Cais families of O Hallinan, O Teahan, O Quinn and many others; and Dallán Forgaill, an early poet whose real name was Eochu Rígéces ('royal poet').

EOCHUCÁN: EOCHAGÁN (och-ag-ān) m, diminutive of *Eochu* (which see).   From this name derives the aristocratic midland surname Meic Eochagáin (Mageoghagan).

EÓGAN: EOGHAN, EOAN (ōn) m, 'born of the yew'.   Eógan is one of the twenty most popular names in early Ireland. Among its bearers were Eógan, ancestor of the Cenél Eógan (the O Neills, Mac Loughlins and other families); Eógan Brecc, ancestor of the Déisi; Eógan Mór, ancestor of the Eóganacht—the early kings of Munster; and Eógan mac Daurthacht, one of the Ulster heroes in the sagas. Among the saints of the name are St Eógan, abbot of Moville, whose feast-day is 31 May; St Eógan of Ardstraw whose feast-day is 23 August; and Eógan, the saintly bishop, whose feast-day is 18 April. In the later middle ages, Eógan was a favourite name amongst the O Donnells of Tír Chonaill and the Mac Sweeneys. As early as the Old Irish period, Eógan was latinised *Eugenius*, a Greek name meaning 'well born', with which it has no connection. It has been anglicised *Owen* (especially among the O Connors of Connacht), *Oyne*, *Oynie* and (by confusion with the borrowed name *Eoin*) *John*. In the south of Ireland, it is generally anglicised *Eugene* and *Gene*. In Scotland Eógan has become *Evan* and *Ewen*.

EÓGANÁN: EOGHANÁN (ōn-ān) m, diminutive of *Eógan* (which see). Eóganán occurs most commonly among the Eóganacht of Munster. There is also a St Eóganán of Assaroe whose feast-day is 20 December. From this name derives the surname Ó hEoghanáin (O Honan),

*EOIN (ōn') m. A borrowing of the biblical name *John* from the Latin form *Joannes*. The name was re-borrowed from the French form *Jehan*, giving in Irish the forms *Seaán*, *Seón, Seóinín* (which see). Amongst the forms in use in the thirteenth century are *Ioan* and *Eoan*.

EOLANG: EOLANN (ō-lang, ō-lan) m. The best-known bearer of this name is St Eolang, patron of Aghabullogue, Co Cork. It has been anglicised *Olan* and is still in use in Aghabullogue.

EÓRANN (ō-ran) f. In Irish story Eórann is wife of Suibne, king of Dál nAraide and hero of *Buile Shuibhne*, which tells how Suibne was cursed by a saint, went mad of terror at the battle of Moira, and spent the rest of his life as a wild birdman wandering through the woods of Ireland.

ERCC, ERC: EARC (ark) m and f. Meaning either 'speckled, dark-red' or 'a salmon'. This is a fairly common name in early pedigrees. There is a St Erc, bishop of Slane, whose feast-day is 2 November. In the Finn-tales, Erc is one of the ladies of the *fian*.

ERCNAT: EARCNAIT (ark-nit') f, diminutive of *Ercc* (which see). St Ercnat is a virginal saint of the north who, in ecclesiastical legend, was dressmaker and embroidress to St Columbcille. Her feast-day is 8 January.

ÉREMÓN: ÉIREAMHÓN (ēr'-a-vōn) m. In the early legendary histories Éremón is the son of the original Goidelic conqueror of Ireland, Míl of Spain. However, the name was revived in the later middle ages and occurs amongst the Meic Suibne (Mac Sweeneys) and some other families. It remained in use as a personal name until the nineteenth century among the Mac Sweeneys but was generally anglicised *Irwin*. Down to the seventeenth century it occurred among the O Hallorans of Galway who anglicised it *Erevan*.

ÉRENNACH: ÉIREANNACH (ēr-an-ach) m and f, 'belonging to the Érainn' an early Irish tribe. This name occurs rarely in the early middle ages. Among its bearers were Érennach, abbot of Leighlin, who died in 774 and Érennach, daughter of Murchad king of Meath.

ÉRIU: ÉIRE (ēr'e) f. Ériu was the ordinary name for Ireland but Ériu was also a goddess and, like other goddess-names, Ériu could be used as a woman's name. Ériu occurs sometimes as a man's name but it may be a different word with a different inflection.

ERNÁN: EARNÁN (arn-ān) m. Perhaps derived from *iarn* 'iron'. Among the saints of the name is St Ernán of Tory whose feast-day is 17 August. It could be anglicised *Ernan*. Ernán has been used to translate the English (originally German) name *Ernest*.

ÉRNE: ÉIRNE (ēr'-n'e) f. In Irish legend Érne is daughter of Búrc Búiredach and Lough Erne is named after her.

ERNÍNE, ERNÉNE: EIRNÍN (ēr'n'-īn') m and f. Perhaps from *iarn* 'iron'. Among the eleven saints of the name are the saintly bishop, Erníne, whose feast-day is 12 May; St Erníne Cass ('curly-haired') of Leighlin, whose feast-day is 23 February; and a female St Erníne whose feast-day is 28 February.

ESCRACH: EASCRACH (as-krach) f. Meaning, perhaps, 'blooming, blossoming'. St Escrach, daughter of Dúnchad, was one of the early saints of north Leinster.

ESNAD: EASNADH (as-na) f, 'musical sound'. In Irish

story Esnad was one of the beautiful but fatal women responsible for the death of the high-king Muirchertach mac Erca. This may not be a genuine personal name.

ÉTAÍN: ÉADAOIN (ēd-īn') f.   Probably connected with *ét* 'jealousy'. O Rahilly believed that Étaín was ultimately a sun-goddess. Étaín is heroine of a fine Old Irish tale, *Tochmar Étaine*, 'The Wooing of Étaín'. Étaín Fholtfhind ('of the fair hair') was daughter of Étar and lived in the fairy dwelling at Howth. Another Étaín, according to the Finntales, gave gifts of gold and silver to St Patrick. There is a St Étaín of the royal race of Connnacht who is patroness of Tumna, Co Roscommon, and whose feast-day is 5 July. Étaín was the name of a daughter of Fínghin Mór Mac Carthaigh, who flourished in the middle of the thirteenth century, and the name occurs among the O Connors, O Haras and O Flannagans in the later middle ages. It appears to have been popularised in England by the opera *The Immortal Hour* (1922).

ETAN: EADAN (ad-an) f.   In the saga literature Etan is Cúchulainn's choice as mistress. Another Etan was daughter of Dian Cécht, the Irish god of healing, and there was also a lady of the Fianna who was called Etan. Of another Etan an early poet wrote satirically:

> I can't tell
> Who will sleep with Etan;
> But this I know
> Fair Etan will not sleep alone.

ETERSCÉL: EIDIRSCÉAL (ed'-ir'-sc'ēl) m.   Perhaps 'messenger, interpreter'. Eterscél is a fairly common name especially in early Munster. Eterscél Már moccu Iair is one of the early Munster heroes and Eterscél mac Maíle hUmai was one of the early kings of Cashel. From this name derives the surname Ó hEidirsceoil (O Driscoll).

ÉTROMMA: ÉADROMA (ēd-rum-a) f, 'light-headedness, giddiness'.   This occurs rarely, as a girl's name in the early period.

ÉVA, ÉBA: ÉABHA (ēv-a) f.   In Irish historical tradition

she was one of the wives of Nemed, legendary invader of Ireland, who according to medieval scholars gave her name to the plain between Benbulben and the sea. In the Finn-tales, she is daughter of Géibtine mac Mórna and was drowned by a wave on the coast of Sligo and gave her name to a headland there.

FACHTNA (facht-na) m and f, 'malicious, hostile'. Fachtna was a relatively common name throughout the country especially in the very early period. According to some traditions Fachtna Fáthach was father of the Ulster king, Conchobar mac Nessa. Among the saints of the name are Fachtna mac Mongaig, patron of the diocese of Ross, whose feast-day is 14 August; the saintly bishop Fachtna whose feast-day is 19 January; and St Fachtna of the shores of Lough Foyle. Fachtna occurs in the later middle ages as a favourite name with the O Farrells and O Mores among whom it became *Festus* and *Festie*. It was latinised *Fantasius*. Fachtna occurs also as a female name.

FACHTNÁN (facht-nān) m, diminutive of *Fachtna* (which see). This name occurs in the early pedigrees of the Uí Briúin Breifne (O Rourkes, O Reillys and other families).

FÁELÁN: FOALÁN (fēl-ān) m, 'wolf'. Fáelán is a common early name especially among the royal families of Leinster. There were three kings of Leinster of the name between the seventh and the ninth centuries. According to the ecclesiastical sources, there were fourteen saints called Fáelán among whom were St Fáelán Find whose feast-day is 5 May; St Fáelán of Meath whose feast-day is 9 January; and St Fáelán, brother of St Fursu, who was martyred in Flanders about 656. According to the Finn-tales, there were ten warriors of the name in the Fianna. One of these, Fáelán mac Finn, was so loyal according to Oisín that he would have rescued Finn from captivity by God. From this name derive the surnames

O Phelan, O Whelan and Hyland.

FÁELCHÚ: FOALCHÚ (fēl-chū) m, 'wolf, wolf-hound'. One of the warriors of the Fianna was called Fáelchú. There is a St Fáelchú whose feast-day is 23 May and Fáelchú was the name borne by the father of St Commán of Ros Commain.

FAIFE (fa-f'e). In Irish saga Faife was the daughter of Ailill and Medb, queen of Connacht.

FAÍLBE: FÁILBHE (fāl'-v'e) m. According to Pokorny this name means 'wolf-slayer' but it could also mean 'lively, sprightly'. Faílbe is an extremely common name especially in Leinster and Munster. Faílbe Fland (†639) was an early king of Munster. Among the many early saints of the name are St Faílbe whose feast-day is 8 April and St Faílbe, abbot of Iona, whose feast-day is 22 March.

FAÍLENN: FAOILEANN (fī-l'an) f.   Meaning, perhaps, 'a graceful woman'. There are two saints of the name: St Faílenn of Uí Fiachrach Aidne (Connacht), whose feast-day is 13 November and St Faílenn, sister of St Colgu of Kilcolgan, whose feast-day is 3 February. According to the historical tradition, Faílenn, a princess of the Déisi, was mother of Eithne, wife of the legendary king of Cashel, Óengus. Another king of Cashel, Faílbe Flann (†637/9), had a daughter called Faílenn.

FAILGE: FAILGHE (fal'-ye) m. The great historical bearer of this name is Russ Failge, son of Catháir Már, legendary ancestor of the Uí Failge (Offaly) from whom descend the O Connors of Leinster. In the fifteenth century this ancestral name was revived as a personal name among the O Connors. It also occurs among the O Dunnes, O Dempseys and O Reillys in the fifteenth and sixteenth centuries.

FAÍLTIGERN: FAOILTIARN (fil'-t'iarn) m, 'lord of wolves'. The only bearer of this name known to me is St Faíltigern whose feast-day is 17 March.

FAIRCHELLACH: FAIRCHEALLACH (far'h'al-ach) m. This name is relatively common in the early period. There is a St Faircheallach of Fore whose feast-day is 10 June. It has been suggested that the surname O Farrelly derives from it.

FAITHLIU, FAITHLENN: FAITHLEANN (fa-l'an) m. This name is attested in the early pedigrees of the Eóganacht and the Dál Cais. There is a St Faithliu, son of Áed Damán, the king of West Munster whose feast-day is 4 June. There is also St Faithliu the deacon whose feast-day is 5 September. The name could be anglicised *Fallon*.

FAINDER: FAINNEAR (fan'-ar) f. Fainder was a female saint of Clonbroney. The name may be a variant of *Ainder* (which see).

FAND: FANN (fon, fown) f. This name may be connected with the Old Irish word *fand* 'a tear'. In Irish mythology Fand was daughter of Áed Abrat and wife of the sea-god, Manannán mac Lir.

FEBAL: FEABHAL (f'av-al) m. Supposed to be connected with Welsh *gwefl* 'lip'. In the Finn-ballads Conn son of Febal was one of the warriors of the Fianna. Another Febal was father of the famous voyager Bran.

FECHÍNE, FECHÍN: FEICHÍN (feh-īn) m. It is possible that two separate names have fallen together here: Fechíne, from *fiach* 'a raven' and Féchín from an old root meaning 'battle'. Fechíne is the name of five Irish saints, the most important of them being St Fechíne of Fore whose feast-day is 20 January. His pet-name is Mo-Ecca and his name has been anglicised as *Festus* and *Festie*. *Fehin* is probably a better English form.

FECHTNACH: FEACHTNACH (f'acht-nach) m, 'happy, prosperous'. This name was borne by an abbot of Fore who died in 781.

FEDACH: FEADHACH, FEÁCH (f'äch) m. Meaning, perhaps, 'dweller in the woods'. Fedach was abbot of Castledermot and died in 876.

FEDELM, FEIDHELM (f'ed-'elm) f. Many famous early Irish women bore this name. Fedelm Fholtebar ('of the smooth hair') is described as 'one of the fair women of Laegaire (Meath)'. Fedelm Fholtchaín ('of the beautiful hair') was daughter of Brión, son of Eochu Mugmedón a legendary king of Connacht, and mother of the two sons of Gabrán, ancestor of the kings of Scotland. Fedelm Noíchrothach ('the nine times beautiful') was a female warrior noted for her great beauty. She was daughter of Conchobar mac Nessa, king of Ulster, and eloped from her husband Cairpre with the great Ulster warrior, Conall Cearnach. According to early sources, there are six saints called Fedelm. St Fedelm and her sister St Mugain were two daughters of the king of Leinster, Ailill mac Dúnlainge. They are patronesses of Tallaght and their feast-day is 9 December. In legend Fedelm was the name of the mother of St Mac Cuilind of Lusk, and Fedelm, grand-daughter of Niall of the Nine Hostages, was mother of St Munnu. The name has been latinised and anglicised *Fidelma*.

FEDELMID, FEIDLIMID: FEIDHLIMIDH, FEIDHLIM (f'ēl'-im'-ī, fē-l'im') m and f.   A very popular name both in the early period and throughout Gaelic Ireland. Among its mythological and legendary bearers are Fedelmid Rechtaid, son of Eochu Mugmedón and ancestor of the Uí Néill; Fedelmid Cris Argaid, son of Túathal Techtmar; and Fedelmid brother of Cumall and uncle of Find. Of the saints of the name are St Fedelmid of Aghalurcher, Co Fermanagh, whose feast-day is 23 December and St Fedelmid of Kilmore, one of the patrons of the diocese, whose feast-day is 3 August. Among its historical bearers were Fedelmid mac Coirpri, Fedelmid mac Tigernaig and Fedelmid mac Crimthainn (†847), three early kings of Munster. In the forms *Feidhlim*, *Féidhlim* it remained popular throughout the later middle ages especially among the O Connors of Connacht, O Donnells, O Neills, O Reillys, Maguires and related families. In the north, it was anglicised as *Felix* generally but *Philip* and *Phelim* were also used. It was also anglicised *Felimy* and *Phelimy*. Fedelmid was in use as a girl's name, but rarely.

*FEIRGIL, FIRGIL m.   A clerical borrowing of the Latin *Virgilius*.

*FELIC m.   A clerical borrowing of the Latin *Felix* 'happy, blessed'.

FEME (f'e-va) f.   Meaning, perhaps, 'a girl, young woman'. The virgin saint, Feme, was sister of Daig mac Cairill of the royal race of the Uí Néill. Her feast-day is 17 September.

FEMMAIR: FEAMAIR (f'am-ir') f.   St Femmair was a virgin saint whose feast-day is 18 January.

*FEORAS (f'ŏr-as) m.   A borrowing from the Anglo-Normans of the French name *Piers*, *Pierre*, the equivalent of English *Peter*. From it derives the surname Mac Fheorais (Corish).

FERADACH: FEARADHACH (f'ar-ad-ach, f'ar-īch) m. This was a relatively common name throughout early medieval Ireland. The name occurs also in the pre-historic period and as a name for early historic kings. Feradach Find Fechtnach was a legendary king of the Picts. Feradach Find mac Duach, an early king of Ossory, was, according to ecclesiastical legend, 'the third king who went to heaven in the time of Columbcille'. According to the Finn-ballads, Feradach was one of the three kings of the British *fianna*. Feradach was a common name among the O Kellys of Connacht in the later middle ages. It was first anglicised *Farreagh* and after latinised *Fergus* and *Fergusius*. It was anglicised *Frederick* among the Mac Donnells of Antrim and other families in Scotland and in the north of Ireland. It was also rendered *Ferdinand* and *Farry*.

FERCHAR: FEARCHAR (f'ar-har) m.   Meaning, perhaps, 'friendly'. Ferchar occurs occasionally in the early period. Ferchar was son of the high-king Niall Frassach. The name has been anglicised *Farquhar* in the Highlands of Scotland. From it derive the modern surnames Fraher, Farraher and Farquhar.

FERCHERTNE (f'ar-ch'art-n'e) m.   In Irish story Ferchertne was a legendary poet. The name was revived in the fifteenth and sixteenth centuries by the learned families of Uí Uiginn (O Higgins) and Uí Chuirnín (O Curneen).

FERDOMNACH: FEARDOMHNACH (f'ar-dow-nach) m. Meaning, perhaps, 'a minor'. Ferdomnach occurs amongst the Airgialla and the Dál Cais. There is a St Ferdomnach of Tuam whose feast-day is 10 June. One Ferdomnach, scholar of Kildare and master of harping, died in 1110.

FERDORCHA: FEARDORCHA (f'ar-dur-cha) m, 'dark man'. This name was common in the sixteenth century and was in use down to recent times. It was latinised *Obscurus*. It has been anglicised as *Frederick* and *Ferdinand* in Ulster— names with which it has of course no connection. As *Dorrie* it was in use in Donegal down to the end of the nineteenth century.

FERGAL: FEARGHAL (f'ar-īl) m, 'valorous'. This was an extremely popular name in early Ireland. It was borne by the high-king Fergal mac Máele Dúin, ancestor of the O Neills, who died in 722. It was a favourite name among the Uí Fearghail (O Farrells) and the Uí Ruairc (O Rourkes). In the nineteenth century, in the forms *Farrell* and *Farall*, it was still in use among the families of O Clerkin, Mac Namee, O Boyle and others but it rapidly became obsolete.

FERGANAINM: FEARGANAINM (f'ar-gan-anm') m, 'anonymous, nameless'. This strange name was fairly common in Ireland down to the early modern period though I know of no very early examples. It was anglicised *Ferdinand*.

FERGUS: FEARGHUS (f'ar-īs) m, 'man-strength'. Fergus has been confused with another old name, Forggus, and after the Old Irish period they are both rendered Fergus. Fergus is an extremely common name in the early period. Among its bearers are Fergus Cerrbél, one of the early kings of the Uí Néill; Fergus mac Róich, one of the great Ulster warriors of the *Táin*; Fergus Scandal, one of the early kings of Munster; and Fergus Tene fo Brega ('fire on Brega'), an early king of Ulster. According to the Finn-ballads, there were ten warriors of the name in the *fian*, one of them being Fergus Fínbél ('Wine mouth'), master of poetry to the *fian*. There is a St Fergus of Iniskeen, on Lough Erne, whose feast-day is 29 March. The name survived even in Co Dublin down to the end of the nineteenth century.

On occasion, it was strangely anglicised *Ferdinand*.

FÉTHCHÚ (f'ē-chū) m. Perhaps from *féth* 'smooth, polished'. There is a St Féthchu whose feast-day is 23 July.

FÉTHMAC (f'ē-vok) m. Perhaps from *féth* 'smooth, polished'. There is a saintly bishop Féthmac of Kiltoom, Co Meath, whose feast-day is 16 March.

FÉTHNAT (f'ē-nit') f. In Irish legend Féthnat was female musician to the Tuatha Dé Danann.

FIACC (f'īak) m. Perhaps a pet-form of *fiach* 'a raven', or pet-form of a name such as *Fiachra* or *Fiachu* (which see). Fiacc was a fairly widely distributed name in the early period. There is a St Fiacc of Sletty whose feast-day is 12 October.

FIACHNA (f'īach-na) m. Perhaps a diminutive of *fiach* 'a raven'. Fiachna was a popular name in the early period. Fiachna mac Delbaíth was an early king of Ireland. Fiachna mac Áeda Róin (†789) and Fiachna mac Ainbítha (†886) were two early kings of Ulster. In Irish legend, Fiachna mac Mongáin is the son of the sea-god, Manannán mac Lir. There is a St Fiachna whose feast-day is 29 April.

FIACHRAE: FIACHRA (f'īach-ra) m. Meaning, perhaps, 'battle-king'. Fiachra is an extremely common early Irish name. Among its bearers are Fiachra Garríne, an early ancestor of the kings of west Munster, and Fiachra, ancestor of the Uí Fiachrach (an early Connacht dynasty) and remote progenitor of the O Dowds, O Clerys, O Hines, O Shaughnessys and other families. Among the saints of the name are St Fiachra abbot of Urard, Co Carlow, whose feast-day is 2 May; St Fiachra abbot of Clonard whose feast-day is 8 February; and the exiled Irish saint Fiachra who settled in Meaux in France and who is venerated as the patron saint of travellers.

FIACHU: FIACHA (f'īach-a) m. A pet-form of *Fiachnae* or *Fiachrae*. This name is borne by a number of early warriors and founders of dynasties. Fiachu Muillethan is the legendary ancestor of the Eóganacht kings of Munster. Fiachu Suigde is legendary ancestor of the Deísi and Fiachu Fidgenid is eponym of the Uí Fidgeinte (O Donovans, O Hehirs, O Kennellys and other families). In the form *Fiacha* it occurs among the O Byrnes of Wicklow and was borne by the famous Feagh Mac Hugh O Byrne. There is a St Fiachu whose feast-day is 27 December. The name has been anglicised *Feagh* but *Festus* was the normal late seventeenth- and eighteenth-century form among the O Kellys and the Burkes.

FIADNAT: FIADHNAIT, FIANAIT (f'ían-it') f, 'wild creature, deer'. There are two saints of the name, one whose feast-day is 4 January and another whose feast-day is 29 November. The name could be anglicised *Feenat*.

FIAL (f'íal) f, 'modest, honourable, generous'. In Irish legend Fial is the wife of Lugaid mac Ítha, legendary founder of the families to which the O Driscolls, O Coffeys and others belong. Fial was also the name of the sister of Emer, Cúchulainn's lover. Fial is the original name of the river Feale and a goddess name.

FIAMUIN: FIAMAIN (f'iav-in') f. Meaning, perhaps, 'swift-footed creature'. Fiamuin was mother of St Berchán of Clonsast.

FIANCHÚ (f'ían-chū) m, 'hound of a warrior band'. A rare early name.

FÍNÁN: FÍONÁN (f'ín-ān) m. There are eleven early Irish saints of this name among whom are St Fínán Cam of Kinnitty and St Fínán of Swords and of Ardfinnan, Co Tipperary, whose feast-day is 16 March.

FINCHÁN: FIONCHÁN (f'un-chān) m. Perhaps, meaning 'hairy, shaggy' or else a diminutive of *Findchad*. A relatively uncommon early name.

FÍNE: FÍONA (f'ín-a) f, 'a vine'. From Latin *vinea*. Fíne was an abbess of Kildare who died in 805. The popular fancy name, *Fiona*, is not a genuine Irish name. It was invented by William Sharp (1855-1905) for his fictional character Fiona Macleod. Presumably he meant it to be a feminine form of *Finn* (*Fionn*) but no such form exists in Irish.

FÍNGIN: FÍNGHIN, FÍNÍN (f'īn'-īn') m, 'wine-birth'. Fíngin mac Áeda, who died in 619, was an early king of Munster and ancestor of the O Sullivans. It was (and, to a degree, is) a favourite name among the Mac Carthys, O Sullivans, O Mahoneys, O Driscolls and other Munster families. There is a St Fíngin whose feast-day is 5 February. The famous Fíngin Mac Carthaig Mór (*c* 1562-1640), a scholar and patron of learning, translated his name as *Florence*. Fíngin was equated with *Florence* as early as the thirteenth century. The name is still common as *Florence*, *Florry*, *Florrie*, and *Flur*.

FINGUINE: FIONGHUINE (f'un-in'-e) m. Meaning, perhaps, 'kin-slayer'. Finguine was a relatively common name in early Ireland with an almost exclusively Leinster-Munster distribution. Finguine mac Con-cen-máthair (†695/6) was an early king of Munster and is ancestor of the Uí Chaím (O Keefes). Finguine mac Láegaire was king of Munster in the beginning of the tenth century. In the later middle ages, the name almost became the exlusive property of the O Keefes.

FÍNMED: FÍNMHIDH (f'īn'-v'i) f. Meaning, perhaps, 'wine-mead'. Fínmed was mother of St Mochuda (Carthage) of Lismore.

FINN: FIONN (f'un) m and f, 'fair, bright white, light-hued'. The most famous bearer of this name is Finn mac Cumaill, hero of the Finn-tales and Finn-ballads, the great hero of Irish popular tradition who is really a Celtic god, *Vindos*. There were three legendary *Finns* associated with Emain Macha, near Armagh. The name also occurs in the Leinster royal genealogies and among the Dál Cais. Finn File mac Rossa Rúaid is a mythical king and poet of the Leinstermen. In the later middle ages, the name remained in use especially among the O Dempseys and the O Driscolls. Finn was also a female name but was relatively uncommon.

FINNABAIR: FIONNABHAIR, FIONNÚIR (f'un-ūr') f.

Meaning, perhaps, 'white ghost, sprite'. In Irish story Finn-abair was daughter of Ailill and Medb, queen of Connacht. Another Finnabair was wife of the Ulster hero Celtchar mac Uithechair. The exact equivalent, *Gwenhwyvar*, occurs in Welsh and in Welsh tradition she is the wife of King Arthur. The Irish name could be anglicised *Fennore*.

FINNACÁN: FIONNAGÁN (f'un-ag-ān) m, diminutive of *Finn* (which see). From it derives the modern surname Ó Fionnagáin (O Finnegan).

FINNÁN: FIONNÁN (f'un-ān) m, a diminutive of *Finn* (which see). There is a St Finnán, bishop of Moville, whose feast-day is 11 February. From this name derives the Connacht surname Ó Fionnáin (O Finan).

FINNBARR: FIONNBHARR (f'un-var) m, 'fair-topped, fair-haired'. There are eight saints of this name. Amongst these are St Finnbarr of Inis Doimle whose feast-day is 4 July; St Finnbarr of Moville; and, the best-known of all, St Finnbarr, patron of the diocese of Cork and traditionally the founder of the early monastery of Cork, whose feast-day is 25 September. The pet-forms *Barre* and *Bairre* occur in the earliest period and are the normal forms of the name of the founder of Cork. The name has been anglicised *Finbar*, *Finnbar* and (like the very similar name *Barrfind*, which see) *Barry*.

FINNCHAD: FIONNCHADH, FIONACHA (f'un-ach-a) m. The equivalent of Gaulish *Vindi-catus* and meaning, perhaps, 'fair battler'. This was a relatively common name especially in the very early period. It was borne by an alleged fifth-century king of Leinster and there is a saintly bishop Finnchad whose feast-day is 16 May.

FINNCHÁEM: FIONNCHAOMH (f'un-chēv) m and f, 'fair, beautiful'. In Irish legend, Finncháem was wife of the great warrior, Cian. Another was mother of the famous Ulster hero, Conall Cearnach while a third Finncháem was wife of Midir and daughter of the king of the fairy-mound, Síd Mónaid, in the east of Scotland. Finncháem occurs very rarely as a man's name.

FINNCHÁN: FIONNCHÁN (f'un-chān) m. Probably a diminutive of a name in *finn-* 'fair' or derived from *finnech* 'hairy'. There is a St Finnchán whose feast-day is 8 November.

FINNCHNES: FINNCHNEAS (f'in'- chn'as) f, 'fair-skinned'. In the Finn-tales Finnchnes is daughter of the king of Uí Chennselaig (South Leinster) and robe-maker to the Fianna.

FINNCHÚ: FIONNCHÚ (f'un-chū) m, 'fair hound, fair warrior'. There was a Finnchú who was abbot of Lismore and who died in 757. The best-known bearer of the name is St Finnchú of Brí Gobann (Mitchelstown) whose feast-day is 25 November. He is still remembered in the area but his name is corrupted to *Fanahan*.

FINNECH, FINDACH: FIONNACH (f'un-ach) m and f. Derived either from *finn* 'fair' or from *finnech* 'having a lot of hair'. St Finnech is patroness of Cell Finnchi, Co Kilkenny, and her feast-day is 2 February. The name also occurs as a man's name in the early period.

FINNEACHT: FINNEACHT (f'in'-acht) f. Derived from *finn* 'fair'. Finnecht was a princess of Meath who was mother of Báethgalach, abbot of Trim (†756), a saint whose feast-day is 5 October. There is a virgin saint Finnecht whose feast-day is 11 August.

FÍNNECHTA, FÍNSNECHTA: FÍNNEACHTA (f'īn'-acht-a). Perhaps a compound of *fín* 'wine' and *snechta* 'snow'. This was a relatively common name in the early period. Fínnechta Fledach (†695) was a high-king but he is also commemorated as a saint whose feast-day is 14 November. Fínnechta mac Cellaig (†939) was abbot of Derry and a distinguished legal scholar while Fínnechta ua Cuill (†960) was an important Munster poet.

FINNÉN: FINNIAN (f'in'-ēn) m. This name is derived from Irish *finn* 'fair, light-hued' with the addition of the British ending *-iaw*. This gives the early Latin form *Vennianus* and such Irish forms as *Finnio* and *Finnian*. It is possible also that *Finnio* came to be considered as a pet-form of names in *Find-* such as Finnbarr. The two most outstanding bearers of this name are St Finnén, bishop of Moville, whose feast-day is 10 September and St Finnén, abbot of Clonard, called 'doctor of wisdom and teacher of the saints of Ireland', whose feast-day is 12 December. The name is generally anglicised *Finnian* and *Finian*.

FINNÉTAN: FINNÉADAN (f'in'-ēd-an) f, 'fair brow'. Finnétan was a lady of the Déisi and ancestress of many nobles of Ossory.

FINNGUALA: FIONNGHUALA, FIONNUALA (f'un-ūal-a) f, 'fair shouldered'. Finnguala was an extremely popular name in Ireland in the later middle ages especially among the O Connors of Connacht, the O Briens, the MacDermotts and other families. The form Finnguala has been almost obsolete since the beginning of the eighteenth century but the shortened form *Nuala*, which has been in existence since at least the thirteenth century, is still popular. It was latinised as *Filorcia* and *Fenollina*. The name has been anglicised as *Flora*, *Penelope*, *Penny*, *Nappy*, and *Fenella* (the Scottish form, made popular by Sir Walter Scott). *Finola*, which has been growing in popularity, is perhaps the best anglicised form.

FINNLUG: FIONNLUGH, FIONNLÚ (f'un-lū) m. A combination of the two god-names, *Finn* and *Lug* (which see). Finnlug was the name borne by the fathers of St Finnén of Clonard and St Brénainn of Clonfert. There are two saints of the name: St Finnlug whose feast-day is 5 June and St Finnlug of Dún Blésce (Doon, Co Limerick) whose feast-day is 3 January.

FINNMAITH: FIONNMHAITH (f'un-va) f, 'fair, good'. Finnmaith was the mother of St Berach. The name could be anglicised *Finnva*.

FINNAT: FINDNAT: FIONNAIT (f'un-it') f. From *finn* 'fair' and meaning 'fair, blonde lady'. There is a St Finnat and Finnat is the name of the mother of St Fintan of Clonenagh. The name could be anglicised *Finnat* or *Fennat*.

FINNSECH: FINNSEACH (f'in'-s'ach) f, 'fair lady, blonde girl'. There are two saints of this name: St Finnsech of Trim whose feast-day is 17 February and St Finnsech of Urney, near Strabane, whose feast-day is 13 October.

FINNSENG: FINNEANG (f'in'-ang) f, 'fair, slim'. A rare early name.

FÍNSCOTH (f'ín-scu) f, 'wine-blossom'. In later saga Fínscoth is daughter of Cúchulainn.

FINTAN: FIONTAN (f'in-tan) m. O Rahilly thought that this name meant 'the white ancient' for in Irish mythology Fintan is credited with having lived for thousands of years. Fintan could also mean 'white fire'. According to an early source, there are seventy-four Irish saints of this name. The best-known of these saints is St Fintan of Clonenagh who is described as the 'head of the monks of all Ireland' and whose feast-day is 17 February. A very similar name, *Fintán*, is considered by some scholars to be a pet-form of a name in *Finn*-such as Finnbarr or Finnchad.

FÍTHEL: FÍTHEAL (f'í-hal) m. Meaning, perhaps, 'a sprite, goblin'. Fíthel was a legendary judge amongst the ancient Irish who could give no false judgment. Fíthel was also the name of a brother of Finn mac Cumaill. Fíthel remained in use amongst the learned family of O Mulconry or Conry by whom it was anglicised *Florence* and *Florry*.

FITHIR (f'i-hir') f. In Irish story Fithir was the daughter of the legendary king Túathal Techtmar.

FLAITHBERTACH: FLAITHBHEARTACH, FLATHAR-TACH (fla-hart-ach) m. This name has been explained as 'bright in sovereignty' but it has generally been understood to mean 'lordly in action, princely'. Amongst the better-known bearers of the name are Flaithbertach mac Inmainéin, king of Munster, who died in 944 and Flaithbertach mac Loingsig, the last king of Cenél Conaill to be high-king, who died in 765. From Flaithbertach mac Eimín, who probably flourished in the tenth century, descend the Uí Fhlaithbertaig (O Flahertys), who once ruled as kings of Connacht. Flaithbertach was a favourite name amongst the Maguires and amongst some other families.

FLAITHEM: FLAITHEAMH (fla-hav) m, 'lord, prince, ruler'. This was a relatively popular name in the south especially in the early period. Flaithem mac Máele-Gaimrid, who died in 1058, is entitled 'chief poet of Ireland'. From this name derives the modern surname Ó Flaithim (Flahive).

FLAITHRÍ (fla-r'í) m.   In the case of Flaithrí, two separate names appear to have fallen together: firstly, *Flathrúa* or *Flaithróe*, meaning, perhaps, 'warrior lord' or some such and secondly, *Flaithrí*, from *flaith* 'ruler, lord' and *rí* 'a king'. This name was relatively common in the early period but it survived into the early modern period. Flaithrí mac Domnaill (†777) was an early king of Connacht. Flaithrí Ó Maolchonaire (*c.* 1560-1629), archbishop of Tuam, was one of the most distinguished Irish ecclesiastics and writers of his time. Among the O Mulconrys, Flaithrí was latinised as *Florentius* and anglicised as *Florence*.

FLANN (flan, flown) m and f, 'bright red, blood red'.   An Old Irish text states that Flann is a name both for men and women. Flann was a very popular early Irish name. Among its bearers were Flann Sinna (†916), one of the high-kings and Flann Feórna (†741), king of Ciarraige and ancestor of the O Connors of Kerry. Flann mac Lonáin (†896) is described as the best poet of the Irish of his day. Flann Mainistrech (†1056) is one of the best-known of the early Irish scholars and Flann ua Cináeda (†1100) was abbot of Trim and principal poet of Meath. Among the saints of the name are St Flann, bishop of Finglas, whose feast-day is 21 January; St Flann mac Fairchellaig, abbot of Lismore, Cork and Emly, whose feast-day is 21 December; and St Flann Finn of Cullen, Co Cork, whose feast-day is 14 January. Among the distinguished women who bore the name are Flann daughter of Donnchad and queen of Ailech, who died in 940 and Flann, daughter of Dúngal and wife of the high-king Malachy I, who died in 890. In the later middle ages, this name was latinised *Florentius* and was later anglicised *Florence*.

FLANNACÁN: FLANNAGÁN (flan-ag-án) m, diminutive from *Flann* (which see). Flannacán mac Cellaig (†896) was king of Brega (Meath) and a poet. From this name comes the modern surname Ó Flannagáin (O Flanagan).

FLANNÁN (flan-án) m, diminutive from *Flann* (which see). The best-known bearer of this name is St Flannán mac

Tairdelbaig of Dál Cais, patron of the diocese of Killaloe, whose feast-day is 18 December.

FLANNAT: FLANNAIT (flan-it′) f, female form of *Flannán* (which see). Flannat was the daughter of the warrior Cuanu mac Ailchíne. She was miraculously cured by St Mochutu of Lismore, became a nun and founded a church on the Blackwater, near Fermoy.

FLANNCHAD: FLANNCHADH, FLANNACHA (flan-ach-a) m. Meaning, perhaps, 'red warrior, battler'. This name was in use among the Eóganacht, Dál Cais and a number of other noble families. From it derives the modern surname, Mac Fhlannchadha (Clancy).

FLIDAIS (fl′id-is′) f. This name seems to contain the word *os* 'a deer'. In Irish story, Flidais is the daughter of Ailill Finn, a Connacht king. She fell in love with the exiled Ulster warrior Fergus mac Róich.

FÓCARTA, FUACARTA: FÓGARTA (fóg-art-a) m, 'one who is proclaimed an outlaw'. Fócarta is in use in the early period especially among the Uí Néill.

FODLA: FODHLA (fõ-la) f. Fodla, who is described as one of 'the shapely women' of the Tuatha Dé Danann, is wife of the god Mac Cécht. In reality, Fodla is another name for Ireland.

FOGARTACH: FOGHARTACH (fõrt-ach) m. Perhaps 'one who inflames'. Fogartach mac Néill, who died in 724, was a high king. The name has often been confused with *Fócarta* (which see).

FORANNÁN, FARANNÁN (fur-an-ãn) m. This is a relatively common name found all over Ireland in the early period. Among the saints of the name are St Forannán of Clonard whose feast-day is 12 February and St Forannán of the Uí Néill whose feast-day is 15 February.

FORBASSACH: FORBHASACH (fur-vas-ach) m, 'battle-watcher, conqueror'. One Forbassach, abbot of Aghaboe, died in 822. The name is long obsolete.

106

FORBFLAITH, FARBHLAIDH: FORLAITH (fur-la) f, 'overlordship, sovereignty'. Forbflaith was daughter of Connla, prince of Teffia, and abbess of Clonbroney near Granard. She died in 780. The name could be anglicised *Farvila*.

FORTCHERN: FOIRTCHEARN (firt'-ch'arn) m, 'overlord'. Exactly the equivalent of *Vortigern*. There is a St Fortchern of Trim whose feast-day is 11 October. It has been suggested that the modern surnames O Fortune, Fortin and Forty derive from this early name.

FOTHUD: FOTHADH (fu-ha) m. This name is probably connected with that of the *Votadini*, a Celtic tribe which lived in Scotland. Fothad is one of the legendary ancestors of the O Driscolls and of the people of Owney (Uaithne). The warrior Fothad Canainne never sat down to a feast without the heads of his slain enemies before him. Fothad Canóne ('of the canon') was an early Irish scholar who died in 819. Fothad was a favourite name among the O Driscolls in the later middle ages.

FRÁECH: FRAOCH (frēch) m. Derived from *fráech* 'heather'. Fráech was the warrior slain in single combat by Cúchulainn. According to saga, Fráech mac Fidaig, a Connachtman, was the most handsome man in all Ireland and Scotland and was the son of the fairy woman Bé Finn.

FRÁECHÁN: FRAOCHÁN (frēch-an) m. Derived from *fráech* 'heather'. In the Finn-ballads Fráechán is a warrior slain by Oscar. There is a St Fráechán of Clonenagh whose feast-day is 20 November. This name was latinised *Broichanus*.

FRÁECHNAT: FRAOCHNAIT (frēch-nit') f. Feminine form of *Fráechán* which occurs rarely as a woman's name.

FRASSACH: FROSSACH (frus-ach) m. Perhaps from *frass* 'shower'. Frassach was an early Irish saint and hermit whose feast-day is 11 April.

FUINCHE: FAINCHE (fin'-he) f. Meaning 'a scald-crow' and probably another name for the Irish goddess of war. There are some fourteen saints of the name. Among these are St

Fuinche of the royal race of the Uí Néill who founded the church of Ros Airthir on Lough Erne and St Fuinche of Clonkee, near Cashel, whose feast-day is 21 January. There is also St Fuinche Garb who seems to be a half-pagan, half-christian character. When threatened with marriage, she dived into Lough Erne and swam away beneath the waters to the sea. She finally re-appeared in Inis Clothrann covered in sea-shells and sea-weed. Fuinche has been anglicised *Fanny*.

FURSU: FURSA (fur-sa) m. The best-known bearer of the name is St Fursu the Pious whose feast-day is 16 June. The name has been anglicised *Fursey*.

ᵹ

GADRA: GADHRA (geir-a) m. A relatively uncommon early name. Gadra mac Dúnadaig (†1027) was an early king of Uí Maine (O Kelly's country). From this name derive the surnames O Gara and Geary.

GÁETH: GAOTH (gē) m, 'clever, wise'. Gáeth is a relatively rare early name.

GÁETHÍNE: GAOITHÍN (gē-hīn) m, diminutive of *Gáeth* (which see). The best-known bearer of this name was Gáethíne, father of Cennétig, the famous battler against the Vikings in the late ninth century. From this name derive the surnames Mac Geehan, Mageean, O Guihan, Guiheen.

GAIMREDÁN: GAIMHREADHÁN (gov'-rān) m, 'wintry person'. This is a relatively uncommon early name.

GALLCHOBAR: GALLCHOBHAR (gal-chŏr) m. Meaning, perhaps, 'lover of foreigners'. A relatively uncommon early name. From this derives the modern surname O Gallchobhair (O Gallagher).

*GARALT: GEARALT (g'ar-alt) m. This name was brought into Ireland by the Anglo-Saxon cleric Garalt of Mayo who died in 732. It was re-introduced to Ireland by the Anglo-Normans where it retained its popularity better than in England.

GARB: GARBH (gorv) m and f, 'rough'. This name was borne by the wife of Demmán mac Cairill (†572), an early king of Ulster. It was also borne by a number of noblemen in the early period.

GARBÁN: GARBHÁN (gorv-ān) m.   From *garb* 'rough'.
This name was borne by some five early Irish saints, the
best-known of them being St Garbán of Cenn Sáile, near
Swords, whose feast-day is 9 July. Garbán mac Énna was an
early king of Munster. From this name derives the modern
surname Ó Garbháin (O Garvan, Garvin). The name could be
anglicised *Garvan* or *Garvin*.

GÉBENNACH: GÉIBHEANNACH (g'ēv'-an-ach, g'ēn'-ach) m,
'captive, prisoner'.   This name was borne by a number of
petty Munster kings in the tenth century. From it derives
the modern surname Ó Géibheannaigh (O Geaney). It could
be modernised *Géannach*.

GELGÉIS: GEILÉIS (g'el'-ēs'), f, 'bright swan'.   In Irish
tradition Gelgéis was daughter of Guaire Aidne, king of
Connacht. Another tradition makes her mother of St Fursu,
the famous Irish missionary who settled in Peronne in France.
It could be anglicised *Gelace*.

*GERÓIT: GEARÓID (g'ar-ōd') m.   This is one of the Irish
forms of the name *Gerald* (from Old German *Gairovald*, a
compound of *ger* 'a spear' and *vald* 'rule') brought into
Ireland by the Anglo-Normans. The other, and perhaps
earlier, form is *Gerald*, *Geralt*. These two forms were considered to be different names in the fifteenth and sixteenth
centuries. In Ireland, this name seems to have been confused
with the similar name, *Gerard*. It remained popular due to
the influence of the FitzGeralds and occurs to this day among
the Flemings, Fitzgeralds, Fitzgibbons and many other
families. The diminutive form *Geróitín*, which is masculine,
not feminine, occurs as early as the thirteenth century. The
modern female name, *Geraldine*, seems to have been invented
by the poet Surrey about 1540 in celebrating the beauty of
Lady Elizabeth FitzGerald, daughter of the ninth earl of
Kildare, and did not become popular until the nineteenth
century.

GERRÓC: GEARRÓG (g'ar-ōg) f.   From *gerr* 'short'.
Gerróc was mother of Cathal Crobderg ('of the wine-red

hand'), king of Connacht, who died in 1224.

GILLA BRÉNAINN: GIOLLA BHRÉNAINN (g'ula vr'ēn-in')
m, 'servant of St Brendan'. This name was borne by an
abbot of Clonfert who died in 1134. It could be anglicised
Gilbrennan.

GILLA BRIGDE: GIOLLA BHRIGHDHE, GIOLLA BHRÍDE
(g'ul-a vr'īd-e) m, 'servant of St Brigid'. A relatively common early name. From this name derive the surnames Mac
Gilbride, Kilbride, MacBride. It could be anglicised *Gilbride.*
The Germanic name *Gilbert* is commonly used in Scotland
as a translation of Gilla Brigde.

GILLA CELLAIG: GIOLLA CHEALLAIGH (g'ul-a ch'al-a)
m, 'servant of St Cellach'. This name was favoured by the
family of O hEidin (Heyne, Hynes) in the later middle ages.
From it derives the surname Mac Giolla Cheallaigh (Mac
Kilkelly, Killikelly). It could be anglicised as *Gilkelly.*

GILLA CÁEMGEIN: GIOLLA CHAOIMHÍN (g'ul-a chiv'-īn')
m, 'servant of St Kevin'. This name occurs only in Leinster
where it was much favoured by the O Tooles. It could be
anglicised *Gilkevin.*

GILLA COMGAILL: GIOLLA CHOMHGHAILL (g'ul-a chōl')
m, 'servant of St Comgall'. Gilla Comgaill Ua Slébéne, principal poet of the north of Ireland, died in 1031. This name
was favoured among the royal families of north Leinster
from whom descend the O Tooles, O Byrnes and others. It
could be anglicised *Gilcole* or *Gilcowal.*

GILLA CRÍST: GIOLLA CHRÍOST (g'ul-a chr'īst) m, 'servant
of Christ'. This name was widely used in Gaelic Ireland and,
in the later middle ages, it was much favoured by the Mac
Dermotts. It has been anglicised *Christian.*

GILLA EPSCOIP: GIOLLA EASPAIG (g'ul-a as-pig') m,
'servant of the bishop'. This may well be an abbreviation of
Gilla Epscoip Eógain 'servant of Bishop Eógan', the well-
known saint of Ardstraw, whose feast-day is 23 August. The
name was extremely popular in the north of Ireland and in
Scotland where it is strangely anglicised as *Archibald.* From

it derives the modern surname Mac Giolla Easpaig (Mac Gillespie, Clusby and Glashby).

GILLA ÍSU: GIOLLA ÍOSA (g'ul-a īs-a) m, 'servant of Jesus'. This name was common among the O Reillys and the Mac Egans in the later middle ages. It survived in Fermanagh down to the early nineteenth century where it was traditionally anglicised *Gilleece*. It has been latinised *Gelasius*.

GILLA MOCHUTU: GIOLLA MOCHUDA (g'ul-a mu-chud-a) m, 'servant of St Mochutu (of Lismore)'. Gilla Mochutu Ua Rebacháin, abbot of Lismore, died in 1129. This name was much favoured by a branch of the O Sullivans who eventually took the surname Mac Giolla Mhochuda (Mac Gillycuddy).

GILLA NA NÁEM: GIOLLA NA NAOMH (g'ul-a na nēv) m, 'servant of the saints'. The best-known bearer of this name was Gilla na Náem Ó Duinn (†1160), scholar of Iniscloghrann on Lough Ree, one of the principal Irishmen of learning of his day. This name was particularly favoured by the learned family of Mac Egan. It was latinised *Nehemias*.

GILLA PÁTRAIC: GIOLLA PHÁDRAIG (g'ul-a fād-rig') m, 'servant of St Patrick'. This name was relatively common in early Ireland, especially in early Leinster, where it gave rise to the surname Mac Gilla Phátraic (now FitzPatrick). O Donovan believed that the now common name *Pádraig*, *Patrick*, which was never used as a man's name in early or medieval Gaelic Ireland, is an abbreviated form of *Gilla Pátraic* or *Gilpatrick*. It is true, however, that *Patrick* was in use among the English colonists in Ireland in the sixteenth and seventeenth centuries.

GILLUCÁN: GILLAGÁN (g'ul-ag-ān) m, 'little lad'. This name occurs occasionally in the early period. From it derives the modern surname Mac Giollagáin (Mac Gilligan, Magilligan, Gillan).

GLAISNE (glas'-n'e) m, a diminutive form of *glas* 'green, grey, grey-blue'. This name was borne by a son of Conchobar mac Nessa, king of Ulster. In the later middle ages, it was a favourite name among the Mac Mahons and Magennises of Ulster and occurs also among the O Reillys. It was latinised

Gelasius. It survived in Ulster down to the middle of the nineteenth century when it was anglicised *James*.

GLASS: GlAS (glos) m, 'green, grey, grey-blue'. Among the famous bearers of this early name are Glass mac Dedaid, a legendary king of Munster, and Glass, son of Nuadu of the Silver Hand, legendary ancestor of the Uí Néill.

GLASSÁN: GLASÁN (glos-ān) m, diminutive of *Glass* (which see). There was a Glassán who was a prince of Ulster in the sixth century. There is also a St Glassán whose feast-day is 1 October.

GOBBÁN: GOBÁN (gub-ān) m. This name is either a pet-form of *goba* 'a smith' or a derivative of *Goibniu* (itself a derivative of *goba*), the name of the ancient Irish god of craftmanship. Gobbán occurs occasionally in the early genealogies and there are some saints of the name. As Gobbán Saor, it is the name of the master-craftsman of Irish folklore.

GOBNAT: GOBNAIT (gub-nit´) f, a feminine form of *Gobbán* (which see). St Gobnat is the patroness of many church-sites in Munster and especially of Ballyvourney and Kilgobnet, Co Kerry, which is named for her. Her feast-day is 11 February. Gobnat is still a popular name in west Munster but it is anglicised *Abigail*, *Abbey*, *Abbie*, *Abina*, *Deborah*, *Debby*, *Dora* and *Webbie*. The forms *Gobnet* and *Gubby* are older anglicisations.

*GOFFRAID: GOFRAIDH, GOFRAIDH, GOFRAÍ (guf-rī) m. This is a borrowing through Old Norse of the Old German name *Godafrid*, from *guda* 'god' and *frithu* 'peace'. It was brought into Ireland by the Vikings and became fairly popular in the later middle ages. It was a favourite name among the family of Ó Catháin (O Kane) in Derry. Goffraid Fionn O Dálaigh was the greatest of the bardic poets. The last bearer of the name in Maghera was Gofraidh Mac Cionnaith who, when dying about 1880, left a curse on any of his race that should revive the name. It survived in Donegal and Derry down to the end of the nineteenth century and was anglicised *Gotty*, *Gorry* and *Geoffrey*.

GORMÁN (gurm-ān) m and f, 'dark, swarthy (of complexion)'.

113

Among the bearers of the name is Gormán Mac Airtrí (†821), king of Munster and ancestor of the O Keeffes. Gormán was also a girl's name.

GORMGILLA: GORMGHIOLLA (gurm-yi-la) m.   From *gorm* 'green, grey' and *gilla* 'lad, gillie'. Gormgilla mac Cenndubáin (†967) was vice-abbot of Clonenagh. This is a very rare name.

GORMLAITH (gurm-la) f.   From *gorm* meaning 'illustrious, splendid' and *flaith* 'sovereignty'. Among the many bearers of this extremely popular early Irish name are Gormlaith, abbess of Clonbroney near Granard, who died in 815; Gormlaith, daughter of Donnchad, who died in 861 and is called 'queen of the Irish' in the annals; Gormlaith, wife of the high-king, Áed Finnliath (†879); Gormlaith, daughter of Flann, wife of the high-king Niall Glúndub (†948); and Gormlaith, daughter of the king of Leinster, wife of Brian Boru and mother of Sitric, king of Dublin who died in 1030. The name retained its popularity throughout the middle ages and in Donegal survived into the nineteenth century in the form *Gormley*. It has been rather oddly anglicised *Barbara* and *Barbary*.

GRÁINNE (grän'-n'e) f.   This name could mean 'she who inspires terror' but O Rahilly has suggested that the name is linked to *grán* 'grain' and considers her to be an ancient corngoddess. In Irish story Gráinne is the daughter of Cormac mac Airt and was betrothed to Finn. She eloped with Diarmait úa Duibne and was pursued by Finn. The name retained its popularity in the later middle ages and was borne by the famous Gráinne or Grace O Malley. The latin form is *Granina*. In the north, the name remained common among the O Duffys, MacNamees, O Gormleys and O Kellys until the nineteenth century when it was generally anglicised *Grace*, an English name derived from Latin *gratia* 'grace'. It has also been anglicised *Gertrude*, *Gertie* and *Grissel(da)*.

GRELLA: GREALLA (gr'al-a) f.   Grealla was the mother of St Manchán of Lemanaghan.

GRELLÁN: GREALLÁN (gr'al-ān) m.   There is a St Grellán

mac Rotáin whose feast-day is 15 April. The name is otherwise uncommon.

GRIAN (gr′ian) f, 'sun, sun-goddess'.   In Irish legend Grian is daughter of Finn and Loch Gréine (Lough Graney, Co Clare) is called after her. According to O Rahilly, she is in fact the Irish sun-goddess.

GUAIRE (gŭar′e) m, 'noble, proud'.   Guaire was a relatively common name in the early period. Among its bearers were Guaire, son of the legendary high-king, Láegaire mac Néill, and Guaire Aidne, king of Connacht, famed in Irish literature as the paragon of generosity. There is a St Guaire of the Bannside who belonged to the royal race of Airgialla (Oriel) and whose feast-day is 9 January.

GÚASACHT (gŭas-acht) m, 'danger, peril'.   There is a St Gúasacht of Granard whose feast-day is 24 January.

GUSS: GUS (gus) m, 'force, vigour, fierceness'.   This very ancient name became obsolete at an early period.

GUSSÁN: GUSÁN (gus-ān) m.   A diminutive of *Guss* which occurs in the early pedigree.

I

IARLAITHE: IARLAITH (īar-la) m.   This is the name of
the patron of the diocese of Tuam whose feast-day is 26
December. Iarlaithe was also the name of the third abbot of
Armagh. It is anglicised *Jarlath*.

IARLUG: IARLUGH (iar-lū) m.   A combination of the
name *Iar* and *Lug*, both probable god-names. St Iarlug was
bishop and abbot of Lismore and his feast-day is 16 January.

IBOR: IOBHAR (iv-ar, ūr) m, 'yew'.   There is a similar
Gaulish name *Eburos*. Among the bearers of this name are
the saintly bishop Ibor who baptised twelve princes of Laois
and St Ibar of Begerin, in Wexford harbour, whose feast-day
is 23 April and who is described in an early text as 'a splendid
flame over a sparkling wave'. It could be anglicised *Ivar*.

IDNAT: IODHNAIT, ÍONAIT (in-it′) f.   Probably meaning
'faithful, pure, sincere'. Idnat was daughter of Flann Redside
and mother of St Finnchú of Brí Gobann (Mitchelstown). It
could be anglicised *Enat* or *Enid*.

IFFERNÁN: IFEARNÁN (if′ar-nān) m.   A relatively rare
early name from which derives the modern Munster surname
Ó hIfearnáin (O Heffernan).

ILLANN: IOLLANN (ul-an) m.   There are a number of
warriors of this name in the Fianna. Illann was also the name
of an early king of Leinster who defeated Óengus, king of
Cashel. Illann was a relatively common name among certain
Irish learned families in the later middle ages.

*ÍMAR: ÍOMHAR (īv-ar) m. This is a borrowing of the Old Norse *Ívarr*. There was an Ímar who was king of Northumbria and of Dublin and the name was borne by a number of Viking leaders in Ireland. The name was soon adopted by the Irish. St Ímar úa hAedagáin, whose feast-day is 13 August, was the teacher of St Malachy at Armagh. From Ímar derives the Clare surname Ó hÍomhair, now rendered Howard. The forms *Ivor* and *Ifor* occur in Britain.

IMCHAD: IOMCHADH ('um-a-cha) m. This name was rather common in the early period but it later became obsolete. There is a St Imchad of the Ardes of Ulster whose feast-day is 25 September.

INDRECHTACH: IONNRACHTACH (un-racht-ach) m. Meaning, perhaps, 'attacker'. This name was relatively common in the eighth and ninth centuries. Indrechtach mac Muiredaig (†723) was an early king of Connacht. There was also an Indrechtach, abbot of Iona, who was martyred on the way to Rome in 854.

*IOSEPH (m). This is a borrowing of the biblical name *Joseph* used exclusively by clerics in pre-Norman Ireland. *Seosamh* is a modern variant form. Its popularity in Ireland dates from the modern growth of devotion to St Joseph.

ÍR: ÍOR (īr') m, 'long, lasting'. In Irish historical tradition, Ír mac Míled is one of the legendary ancestors of the Irish. This name comes into favour again among the Meic Raignaill (Reynolds) in the later middle ages.

IRÉL, IRIAL (ir'-īal) m. In Irish story, Irél is son of the great Ulster warrior, Conall Cearnach. Irél Glúmar is one of the remote legendary ancestors of some Irish families and in the later middle ages the name was revived among such families as the O Farrells of Longford, O Loughlins of the Burren, Mac Mahons of Oriel and, on occasion, the O Reillys of Breifne.

ÍTE: ÍDE (īd'-e) f. St Íte is a saint of the Déisi, patroness of Kileedy, Co Limerick, whose feast-day is 15 January. According to legend, she fostered the child Jesus and the early writer Oengus calls her 'the bright sun of the women of Munster'. The name survived in Donegal until the end of the nineteenth century but it has been anglicised *Ita* and *Ida*. *Míde* is an early pet-form of Íte which could be rendered *Meeda* in English.

IUCHRA (uch-ra) f. In the Finn-ballads Iuchra is the daughter of Ábartach who turns her rival, Aífe, into a heron.

L

LABRAID: LABHRAIDH (low-rī) m, 'speaker'. Labraid Longsech is the legendary ancestor of the Leinstermen and it is clear that he is regarded as a god. Labraid is also the name of a number of other legendary personages in early Irish story. Labraid of the Red Hand is one of the heroes of the Fianna who accompanied Oscar overseas. The name was also borne by christian clerics as, for example, Labraid, abbot of Slane, who died in 845.

LACHTÍNE, LACHTÉNE: LACHTÍN (locht-ín') m. Derived from *lacht* 'milk' and probably meaning 'milk-like' 'milk-coloured'. The best known bearer of this name is St Lachtíne of Achad Úr (Freshford, Co Kilkenny), whose feast-day is 19 March. According to some traditions, he is considered the protector of the Munstermen.

LACHTNAE: LACHTNA (locht-na) m, 'milk-like, of the colour of milk'. Lachtna is found principally in Munster and is the name of a number of early Munster kings and nobles, including the brother and great-grandfather of Brian Boru. It was anglicised *Lucius* which remained an extremely popular name among the O Briens down to modern times. In the nineteenth century, Lucius was re-gaelicised *Laoiseach* (see Laígsech).

LACHTNÁN, LACHTNÉNE: LACHTNÁN (locht-nān) m, a diminutive of *Lachtna* (which see). This name was relatively common in the early period but it occurs rarely after the twelfth century. Lachtnán mac Mochthigern (†875) was bishop of Kildare and abbot of Ferns. From this name derives the surname Ó Lachtnáin (O Loughnane, Lawton).

LÁEBÁN: LAOBHÁN (lēv-ān) m, 'crooked, oblique'. There are two saints of this name: St Láebán whose feast-day is 9 August and St Láebán of Áth Aguis whose feast-day is 1 June.

LÁECHRÍ: LAOCHRA (lēch-ra) m, 'king of warriors'. A rare early name.

LÁEGAIRE: LAOGHAIRE, LAOIRE (lē-r'e) m, meaning, probably, 'calf-herd'. Láegaire is one of the more common early personal names. Among its bearers are Láegaire mac Néill, early historic king of Tara; Láegaire Bern Buadach, legendary ancestor of the men of Ossory; and Láegaire Lorc, legendary ancestor of the Leinstermen. There are two saints of the name: St Láegaire, whose feast-day is 11 May and St Láegaire of Lough Conn. From this name derives the modern surname Ó Laoghaire (O Leary).

LAIDCENN, LAIDGENN: LAIDHGEANN (lī-g'an) m, 'snow-head'. Laidcenn mac Bairceda was one of the most famous of the early poets. Among the saints of the name are St Laidcenn, abbot of Clonfertmulloe, one of the great scholars of his day, whose feast-day is 12 January.

LAÍDECH: LAOIDHEACH (lī-ach) m, 'songful, poetical'. Laídech was father of St Cainnech (Canice) and is described as a 'venerable poet'.

LAIGNECH: LAIGHNEACH (lein-ach) m, 'a Leinsterman'. This was the name of the father of St Abbán. This name occurs among the Mageoghagans and the O Maoileachlainns in the later middle ages. It is identical with the modern surname Lynagh and indeed could be anglicised *Lynagh*.

LAÍGSECH: LAOIGHSEACH, LAOISEACH (līs'-ach) m, 'man of Laois'. This was a favourite name among the O Mores of Laois and also occurs among the O Farrells. It has been anglicised *Lucius*, *Lewis* and *Louis* but the form *Lysagh* is more correct.

LÁIMSECH: LÁIMHSEACH (lāv'-s'ach) f. Láimsech was

an early female saint of Leinster.

LAISRE (los'-r'e) m.   From *lassar* 'flame, fire'. This name occurs chiefly in Munster in the early period.

LAISRÉN, LAISREÁN (los'-r'ān) m, diminutive of *Laisre* (which see).   Among the saints of the name are Laisrén of Devenish (better known as Molaisse) whose feast-day is 12 September; St Laisrén, third abbot of Iona, whose feast-day is 16 September; and St Laisrén of Innismurray whose feast-day is 12 August. This name has been anglicised *Laserian* and, more curiously, *Lazarus*, in the north.

LAITHCHE (la-he) f.   St Laithche was one of the two nuns who were the companions of St Cranat of Fermoy.

LALLÓC: LALÓG (lal-ōg) f.   St Lallóc was a virgin saint, daughter of Dar Erca and supposed niece of St Patrick in Irish tradition.

LASSAR: LASAIR (los-ir') f, 'flame, fire'.   This is a relatively common female name in early Ireland. Lassar was daughter of Láegaire mac Néill, an early king of Tara. Lassar of the Déisi of Brega (Meath) was mother of bishop Ibar and of many other saints. St Lassar, a nun of Achad Durbcon (probably Macroom) is traditionally supposed to have been a pupil of St Finnbarr of Cork. There is also a St Lassar, a virginal saint of Meath, whose feast-day is 18 February.

LASSAR FHÍNA: LASAIRÍONA (los-ir'-īn-a) f, 'fire of wine'.   This was a very popular name in Connacht in the later middle ages where it was borne by ladies of the O Hanleys, Mac Donaghs, Mac Dermotts, O Beirnes and others. It has been anglicised *Lassarina* but *Lasrina* is the commonest form.

LEBARCHAM: LEABHARCHAM (lowr-cham) f, 'slender, stooped'.   In Irish story Lebarcham is the nurse of the tragic heroine Deirdre. Lebarcham was also the name of one of Cúchulainn's lovers.

LEDBÁN: LEADHBHÁN (l'ei-vān) m, 'plaintive'.   This relatively rare name occurs in the early genealogies.

LENNÁN: LEANNÁN (l'an-ān) m, 'lover, sweetheart, paramour'. This name occurs especially in the early genealogies of the Clare dynastic families, Corcu Baiscinn. Lennán mac Cathrannach was king of Corcu Baiscinn from 898 to 915. From it derives the modern surname Ó Leannáin (O Linnane, Lennon, Leonard). The name could be anglicised *Lennan*.

LERBEN: LEARBHEAN (l'ar-van) f. Meaning, perhaps, 'lady of the sea'. Lerben Bán was abbess of Clonbroney, Co Roscommon, and died in 794.

LÍADAN, LÍADAIN, LÍADAINE (l'ía-dan') f. Meaning, perhaps, 'grey lady'. Líadan was the beloved of the poet Cuirithir and was a poetess herself. When Cuirithir came to love her, she was already a nun. He became a monk and, like Abelard and Heloise, they remained lovers. Líadan was also the name of the mother of St Ciarán of Seir. According to legend, when she was asleep in her bed, she turned her face to heaven and a star fell into her mouth and in this way she conceived Ciarán. Líadan is also the name of one of the patron saints of the Dál Cais.

LÍADNÁN: LIADHNÁN (l'ian-ān) m. Meaning, perhaps, 'grey lad'. There are two saints of this name, the best-known being St Líadnán of Fore whose feast-day is 5 February. The name could be anglicised *Leanan*.

LIAMUIN: LIAMHAIN (l'iav-in') f. Meaning, perhaps, 'comely'. In Irish tradition Liamuin is believed to be the sister of St Patrick.

LÍ BAN: LÍ BHAN, LÍOBHAN (l'í-von) f, 'beauty of women'. In the Ulster tales, Lí Ban is wife of Lúathlám. Lí Ban is also another name for a remarkable half-pagan, half-christian personage called *Muirgein* (which see).

*LIBER m. This is probably a borrowing from Latin *liber* 'free'. The name is largely clerical and according to an early source there are eighteen saints of the name. There was a Liber who was abbot of Aghaboe and who died in 620. The diminutive *Librén* also occurs.

LIFE (l'i-f'e) f. According to medieval tradition a lady called Life gave her name to the river Liffey. However, Life seems to have been the old name for the vale of the Liffey and *abha Lifi* the older name of the river. This latter name has been rendered *Annalivia* by James Joyce.

LÍGACH: LÍOGHACH, LÍOCH (l'ïg-ach, l'ïch) f, 'lustrous, beautiful'. Lígach was daughter of the high-king Flann mac Maíl Sechnaill (†916) and wife of Congalach, another high-king.

LÍTHGEN: LÍTHGHEIN (lï'-in') m. From *líth* 'festival, luck, prosperity' and *gein* 'birth'. There is an exactly equivalent Gaulish name, *Litogeni*. There is a St Líthgen of Offaly whose feast-day is 16 January.

LÓCH, LÚACH (lōch) m and f, 'bright, radiant'. Cognate with *lóchet* 'lightning'. Lóch Mór mac Ma-Femis is the mythological ancestor of the kings of Munster. In the Finn-ballads, Lóch is daughter of the legendary warrior Mac Niad and mother of the equally legendary poet, Nuadu Finn Éces. In reality, Lóch is a pagan divinity.

LÓCHÍNE, LÓCHÉNE: LÓCHÁN, LUACHÁN (lōch-ān lūach-ān) m, a diminutive of *Lóch* 'radiant, splendid'. There is a St Lóchéne of Cong whose feast-day is 17 April. Lóchíne Mend was one of the best scribes among the Irish. Lóchán was a saint of the Leinstermen, and the father of St Colmán of Meath was also called Lóchán.

LOCHLAINN (luch-lin') m. Meaning, probably, 'Viking'. This name came into use in the early middle ages among the Uí Néill of the north and other families. In the later middle ages, it was favoured by the O Hanleys of Connacht, the Mac Cabes, and other families. Until the nineteenth century it was in use among many northern families—O Hoey, O Haughey, O Connellan, Malone, Mac Creesh, Mac Cann, Mac Teague, Mac Namee and Mac Kenna—but it is now rare or obsolete. It was 'translated' *Laurence* among the O Kellys in the second half of the seventeenth century. It has been anglicised *Loughlin* and *Laughlin*. In Scotland it is much used by the families of McIntosh and McLean in the form *Lachlan*.

LOIMSECH: LOIMSEACH (lim'-s'ach) f. From *lomm*

'bare'. St Loimsech is an early saint of the Leinstermen.

LOINGSECH: LOINSEACH (lin'-s'ach) m, 'seafarer, exile'. Loingsech was a relatively common name in the early period. Loingsech mac Máil Pátraic (†989) was scholar of Clonmacnoise and Loingsech mac Lonáin (†1012) was abbot of Roscrea. From it derives the modern surname Ó Loingsigh (Lynch).

LOMMÁN: LOMÁN (lum-ān) m. From *lomm* 'bare'. Among the saints of this name are St Lommán of Lough Owel, of the royal race of the Uí Néill, whose feast-day is 7 February; St Lommán of Lough Gill, of the royal race of Oriel, whose feast-day is 4 February; and St Lommán of Trim, supposed in Irish tradition to be the nephew of St Patrick, whose feast-day is 11 October. The name has been anglicised *Loman*.

LONÁN (lun-ān) m. From *lon* 'blackbird'. Irish tradition says that there are eleven saints of this name. Among them are St Lonán Finn whose feast-day is 22 January; St Lonán whose feast-day is 6 June; and St Lonán of Trevet in Meath whose feast-day is 1 November.

LONNGARGÁN: LONARGÁN (lun-arg-ān) m. From *lonn* 'bold, eager' and *garg* 'rough, fierce'. This name is found chiefly among the Dál Cais and from it derives the modern surname Ó Lonargáin (Londragan, Lonergan).

LONNÓG (lun-ōg) f. From *lonn* 'bold, eager'. Lonnóg was the lady who was kind to Suibne Gelt (Mad Sweeney), the wild bird-man of Irish story.

LORCCÁN: LORCÁN (lurk-ān) m. From *lorcc* 'silent' or 'fierce'. This was a very common name in early medieval Ireland and was borne by a number of kings. Lorccán was grandfather of Brian Boru. Lorccán mac Cellaig was a tenth-century king of Munster whilst two kings of Leinster in the ninth and tenth centuries, bore the name. It was also the name of Lorcán Ó Tuathail (more commonly known as Laurence O Toole) the saintly archbishop of Dublin whose feast-day is 14 November. The name has been anglicised *Laurence*, a name of Latin origin with which it has no connection. *Lorcan* is a more acceptable English form.

LÚARÁN (lŭar-ān) m.   Perhaps from *lúar* 'fierce'. St Lúarán is the patron saint of Derryloran, near Cookstown. His feast-day is 29 October. The name could be anglicised *Loran*.

*LÚCÁS m.   The biblical name, *Luke*, which was favoured by the learned family of MacEgan in the later middle ages.

LUG: LUGH (lŭ) m, 'light, brightness'.   Lug is a Celtic god, son of the goddess Eithne. In Welsh he is known as Lleu and in Irish tradition he is the *Samildánach* 'master of all the arts'.

LUGACH: LUGHACH (lŭ-ach) f.   Perhaps derived from *Lug* (which see).   In the Finn-ballads Lugach is daughter of Finn.

LUGÁED: LUGHAODH (lŭ-ē) m.   A combination of the god-names *Lug* and *Áed* (which see).   Lugáed was a saint of Meath whose feast-day is 31 January.

LUGAID: LUGHAIDH, LÚÍ (lŭ-ī) m, derived from *Lug* (which see).   Lugaid is perhaps the seventh most popular name in early Ireland. Lugaid Loígde is the legendary ancestor of the O Driscolls, O Coffeys and related families while his brother, Lugaid Laígne, is regarded as the ancestor of the O Mores and related families. Lugaid mac Con is an early warrior from the south of Ireland while Lugaid Mend is a legendary ancestor of the Dál Cais. Among the many saints of the name are St Lugaid moccu Óchae (better known as Molua), who died in the early seventh century and St Lugaid of Breifne whose feast-day is 12 February. Lugaid remained a favourite name in the Irish learned family of O Clery who anglicised it as *Lewy* and *Lewis*. It has also been rendered *Louis* and *Aloysius*.

LUGÁN: LUGHÁN (lŭ-ān) m, a diminutive of *Lug*.   Lugán is one of the remote ancestors of the Maguires and related families. There is a St Lugán whose feast-day is 16 August.

LUGNA: LUGHNA (lŭ-na) m, a diminutive of *Lug* (which see).   St Lugna was a disciple of St Patrick who settled near Lough Mask. Lugna is a rare early name which soon became obsolete.

LUGTHIGERN: LUIGHTHIGHEARN, LÚITHIARN (lŭ-hiarn) m. A compound of *Lug* (which see) and *tigern* 'a lord'. Lugthigern is a saint of Tomfinlough, Co Clare, whose feast-day is 28 April. Otherwise the name is very rare.

LUIGSECH: LUIGHSEACH, LUÍSEACH (lī-s'ach) f. A feminine form derived from *Lug* which means 'radiant girl'. St Luigsech was a virgin saint whose feast-day is 22 May. This name has been anglicised *Lucy*.

m

MAC BETHAD: MAC BEATHA (mok b'a-ha) m, 'a son of life, a righteous man'.   This name originally meant a professed cleric. Among its bearers were Mac Bethad mac Ainmere, principal judge of Armagh, who died in 1041 and Mac Bethad Ua hAilgenáin, abbot of Cork, who died in 1106. It was greatly favoured by the O Connors of Kerry in the eleventh and twelfth centuries. It is anglicised *Macbeth* and is, of course, identical with the Macbeth of Shakespeare's play.

MAC CAILLE: MAC COILLE (mok kil'-e) m, 'son of the wood'.   This is the name of a saintly bishop whose feast-day is 25 April and who was supposed, in later legend, to be the son of St Patrick's sister, Darerca.

MAC CÁIRTHINN (mok kār'-hin') m, 'son of the rowan tree'.   This is a relatively uncommon early name, the most famous bearer of it being St Mac Cáirthinn, patron saint of Clogher, whose feast-day is 15 August. It has been anglicised *Macartan* and has achieved some popularity in modern times.

MAC CON (mok-kun) m, 'son of a wolf'.   Mac Con is one of the early divine personages in the origin-stories and is regarded as ancestor of the O Driscolls, O Coffeys, O Broders or Brodericks, O Cullinanes and related families. Mac Con was a favourite name amongst the O Driscolls, MacNamaras and other families in the later middle ages and is still in use, in the form *Maccon*, among certain families in Co Clare.

MAC CUILIND, MAC CUILINN (mok-kil'in') m, 'son of the holly'.   Mac Cuilind was a saintly abbot of Lusc whose feast-

127

day is 6 September.

MAC DARA (mok-da-ra) m, 'son of the oak'. A relatively rare early name. There is a St Mac Dara who is the object of popular devotion in Connemara and is regarded as patron by the fishermen.

MAC LAISRE (mok-los'-r'a) m, 'son of flame'. In the early period this name occurs chiefly in Leinster and Munster. There is a St Mac Laisre who was abbot and bishop of Armagh and who died in 624. His feast-day is 12 September. Another Mac Laisre was abbot of Bangor and died in 647.

MAC NISSE (mok-n'is'-e), m, 'son of Ness (perhaps a goddess)'. There are two well-known saints of the name: St Mac Nisse, abbot of Clonmacnoise, whose feast-day is 13 June; and the better known St Mac Nisse of Connor whose feast-day is 3 September.

MAC RAITH (mok-ra) m, 'son of grace'. This early name has a Munster-Leinster distribution and was especially favoured by west Munster peoples in the early period. From it derives the surname Magrath.

MAC TÁIL (mok-tal') m, 'son of adze'. The best-known bearer of this name is St Mac Táil of Kilcullen whose feast-day is 11 June.

MACHA (moch-a) f. In Irish legend Macha is one of the three war-goddesses of the Tuatha Dé Danann. Another Macha is called 'Macha of the red hair' and from her Emain Macha (Navan fort, near Armagh) and Ard Macha (Armagh) are named. There is also a St Macha, one of the daughters of Lénine and patroness of Killiney, whose feast-day is 6 February.

MÁEDÓC: MAODHÓG (mē-ōg) m, a pet-form of *Áed* (which see). Among the saints of this name are St Máedóc of Clontooskert, near Ballinasloe, whose feast-day is 18 March; St Máedóc of Lismore whose feast-day is 29 December; and, perhaps the best-known of all, St Máedóc of Ferns who was born in Templeport, Co Cavan, and who is thus the patron-saint both of the south Leinstermen and the men of Breifne.

In the nineteenth century, in the families of O Doyle, Kavanagh and other south Leinster families the name was translated *Moses* among Catholics, and *Aiden* among Protestants. In Cavan and especially in Templeport the form *Aidan* is preferred generally and neither *Moses* nor the common local anglicised form, *Mogue*, are in use as personal names.

MÁEL ANFAID: MAOLANAITHE (mēl-an-a-ha) m, 'devotee of the storm'. This name fell into disuse at an early period. There is a St Máel Anfaid of Molana, near Lismore, whose feast-day is 31 January.

MÁEL COLUIM: MAOLCHOLUIM (mēl-chul-im') m, 'servant of St Colmcille'. This name occurs occasionally in Ireland but it was especially popular in Scotland where it was favoured by the royal dynasty. It has been anglicised *Malcolm*.

MÁEL DÚIN: MAOL DÚIN (mēl dūn') m. Possibly a reformation of Celtic *duno-maglos* 'warrior of the *dún* (fortress)'. This name was relatively common in early Irish society. Máel Dúin was father of the famous high-king, Fergal mac Máele Dúin (†722) and Máel Dúin mac Áeda Bennáin was an early king of west Munster. From this name derives the modern surname Ó Maoldúin (O Muldoon).

MÁEL EOIN: MAOL EOIN (mēl ōn') m, 'devotee of St John'. There is a saintly bishop Máel Eoin whose feast-day is 20 October. From this name derives the modern surname Ó Maoileoin (O Malone).

MÁEL ÍSU: MAOL ÍOSA (mēl īs-a) m, 'devotee of Jesus'. This early name spread from clerical circles into lay society. Among its well-known bearers are Máel Ísu mac Amalgada, abbot of Armagh (†1091) and Máel Ísu mac Flannabrat, abbot of Inis Cathaig (†997). Máel Ísu ua Brolcháin, who died in 1086 and is described as a 'master of wisdom and piety' in the annals, was one of the finest religious lyric poets of early medieval Ireland.

MÁEL MÁEDÓC: MAOLMHAODHÓG (mēl vē-ōg) m, 'devotee of St Máedóc'. The most famous bearer of this name is St Máel Máedóc Ó Morgair, better known as St Malachy of Armagh, the notable twelfth-century reformer

129

of the Irish church and friend of St Bernard. His feast-day is 3 November. The name has usually been latinised *Malachias* and anglicised *Malachy*.

MÁEL MÓRDA: MAOL MHÓRDHA (mēl vōr-a) m. From *mórda* 'great, haughty'. This was a favourite name amongst the early Leinstermen and was borne by a number of their kings. In the later middle ages, it was especially favoured by the O Dempseys, O Reillys and Mac Sweeneys. It has generally been anglicised *Myles* among the O Reillys.

MÁEL MUAD: MAOL MHUADH (mēl vūa) m. From *muad* meaning, perhaps, 'noble, proud'. The best-known bearer of this name is Máel Muad mac Brain, king of Desmond (†978) and ancestor of the O Mahoneys. Máel Muad was a favoured name among the O Mahoneys in the later middle ages. It was anglicised *Mealmoe* and, later, *Molloy*.

MÁEL MUIRE: MAOL MHUIRE (mēl vir'-e) m and f, 'devotee of Mary'. Among the bearers of this name are St Máel Muire ua Gormáin, author of a martyrology of the Irish saints, whose feast-day is 3 July. His name is generally latinised as *Marianus*. Máel Muire was a favourite name among the Mac Sweeneys and also occurs commonly amongst the Magraths. It survived in south east Ulster down to the nineteenth century. It was anglicised *Murray*, *Miles*, *Milo*, *Meyler* and *Myles*. Máel Muire occurs frequently as a girl's name. Máel Muire was one of the wives of the high-king Áed Finnliath (†879) and mother of the high-king Niall Glúndub (†919). Niall Glúndub himself had a daughter Máel Muire who died in 966. Another Máel Muire was daughter of Amlaíb, king of Dublin, and wife of the high-king Máel Sechnaill II.

MÁEL ODRÁN: MAOL ODHRÁIN, MAOLÓRÁIN (mēl ōr-ān') m, 'devotee of St Odrán. There are two saints of this name: St Máel Odrán whose feast-day is 28 May and St Máel Odrán of Slane whose feast-day is 31 May.

MÁEL RUANAID: MAOLRUANAIDH, MAOLRUANAÍ (mēl rūan-ī) m. Perhaps from *ruanaid* 'a champion, a strong man'. Máel Ruanaid mac Donnchada (†843) was king of

Meath while Máel Ruanaid mac Flainn (†901) was claimant to the kingship of Tara. In the later middle ages, Máel Ruanaid was a favourite name among the O Carrolls of Éile and among the O Mulrooneys, Mac Donaghs and Mac Dermotts of Connacht. It was latinised *Morrianus* and *Murianus*. It was anglicised *Mulroney* among the O Carrolls and others but it became *Myles* among the Mac Dermotts.

MÁEL SECHNAILL,MÁEL SECHLAINN: MÁELECHLAINN M'LACHLAINN (mēl-ach-lin', mlach-lin') m, 'devotee of St Sechnall'. This was a favourite name among the dynasties of Meath and was borne by two famous high-kings: Máel Sechnaill mac Máel Ruanaid who died in 862 and his descendant, Máel Sechnaill Mór mac Domnaill, who died in 1022. Both of these are better known as *Malachy*. It was one of the commonest names in the later middle ages and was greatly favoured by the O Flanagans and the O Kellys. It survived among the Mac Canns, Mac Ardles, O Morgans, Mac Enealises and other northern families until the later nineteenth century. In Omeath *Lochaigh* was a by-form of the name.

MÁELÁN: MAOLÁN (mēl-ān) m, 'a warrior'. Máelán, lector of Kells, 'the wisest of all the Irish' died in 1050. This name occurs occasionally in the early pedigrees. From it derives the modern surname, Ó Maoláin (O Mullan, Mullins).

MÁEN: MAON (mēn) m and f, 'silent'. A by-name for one of the principal Irish pagan gods. In the earliest mythology it occurs as a god-name but it is more frequently a female name in the legendary material. Máen was daughter of Conn Cétchathach ('of the Hundred Battles'). Another Máen was daughter of the king of Ulaid and mother of the legendary judge Morann.

MÁENACH: MAONACH (mēn-ach) m. From *Máen* (which see). Máenach was one of the more common early Irish names and is very widely distributed. There is a St Máenach who was abbot of Dunleer. Máenach mac Siadail, abbot of Bangor (†921), is described in the annals as one of the most distinguished scholars in the Ireland of his day. From Máenach derives the modern Irish surname Ó Maonaigh (O Mooney). It was in use among the O Flahertys down to the seventeenth century.

*MAGNUS: MACHNUS, MÁNUS (mān-as) m. From Latin *magnus* 'great'. This name was borrowed from the Norse, who in turn borrowed it from the Latin Carolus Magnus (Charlemagne, the great emperor of the Franks) possibly in the eleventh century. In Ireland it did not become popular until the late twelfth century. In the later middle ages it was particularly favoured by the Mageraghtys, Maguires, Magoverns and O Donnells. Down to the late nineteenth century it was still popular in the north among the O Donnells, Mac Faddens, Mac Enealises, Wards, Mac Gineleys and in several families in south Armagh and Monaghan. It was also common in Derry among the O Kanes, MacNicholls and Mac Closkeys. It was anglicised as *Manasses* and *Moses* in the nineteenth century but it is best rendered *Manus*. It was latinised *Maganius*.

MAÍLÍN: MAOILÍN (mīl-ín´) m. Probably related to *Máelán* (which see). This name was much favoured by the learned family of Ó Maolchonaire (O Mulconry, Conry) in the later middle ages.

MAINCHÍNE: MAINCHÍN (man´-hīn´) m, diminutive from *manach* 'a monk'. Of the saints of the name are St Mainchíne the Wise of Laígis whose feast-day is 2 January and St Mainchíne of Limerick, one of the patron saints of Dál Cais. This name has been anglicised *Munchin* and *Mannix*.

MAINE (man´-e) m. This was an extremely popular early name borne by many legendary warriors and founders of dynasties. Maine Cerbba was legendary ancestor of many Munster peoples including the O Donovans, O Kennellys and O Scanlans; Maine mac Néill was legendary ancestor of an important branch of the Uí Néill which includes the Foxes, Mac Breens, O Kirlehans, Magawleys and the learned family of Ó Maolchonaire (Conry); and Maine Mílbél ('Honeymouth') was a legendary Munster hero. According to the Finn-tales, Maine was also the name of one of the warriors of the *fianna*. There is also a St Maine whose feast-day is 2 September. Maine was in use as a personal name among the families of Mac Brannan, O Caherny, O Kelly and especially the Mac Breens of Brawney in the later middle ages. It was anglicised *Many*.

*MÁIRE (mār'-e) f. A borrowing of the name Mary. Máire is extremely rare in the period before the seventeenth century though it occurs as the name of a lady of the Bissetts of the Glynns of Antrim in the fourteenth century and occasionally among the Mac Sweeneys and the Burkes in the sixteenth century. In Ireland, as in western Europe generally in the early period, the name of the Virgin Mary was considered too sacred to be used as a personal name. The early Irish used the forms *Gilla Muire* 'servant of Mary' and *Máel Muire* 'devotee of Mary'. As in Spain attributes of the Virgin Mary, e.g. *Dolores*, *Asunción*, *Mercedes* etc., were used rather than the name itself. In England, Mary lost popularity after the reformation but by the middle of the eighteenth century it had come back into favour and one in every five female children was baptised Mary. In Ireland there were very few Marys until relatively recent times thought at present about one in four of the women of Ireland bear the name. This can be explained by the fact that the most popular of all late medieval and early modern female names, *Mór* (which see), was invariably anglicised *Mary* in the nineteenth century. The following Irish pet-forms of Máire were (or are still) in use: *Maille*, *Mailse*, *Mailti* (these latter being rendered *Marjory* and *Margery* as well as *Molly*), *Mallaidh*, *Máirín* and *Méars* (in use in Kerry until recently). Among the forms in use in English are *Moira*, *Moyra*, *Maura*, *Maureen*, *May*, *Molly*, *Moll*, *Mamie* and, latterly, the continental forms *Maria* and *Marie*.

MAITHGEN: MAITHGHEN, MAITHÍN (ma-hīn') m, 'son of the bear'. A very rare early Irish name which also occurs in Gaulish.

*MAIÚ, MAIDIÚ m. A borrowing of the biblical name *Matthew* which occurs among the Anglo-Norman settlers in Ireland. There is a diminutive form *Maidiucc* from which derives the modern surname Maddock. The latter was adopted by a branch of the MacMurroughs. *Maitiú* is now in general use as an Irish form of *Matthew* though *Matha*, probably a native form of independent origin, was also in use.

MANCHÁN (mon-chān) m, diminutive of *manach* 'a monk'. According to an early text there are some eight saints of this name. Among them are St Manchán of Mohill, Co Leitrim, whose feast-day is 14 February; St Manchán of Delvin in Co Westmeath whose feast-day is 24 March; and the best-known of all, St Manchán of Liath Mancháin (Lemanaghan, Co Offaly) whose feast-day is 24 January.

MARCÁN (mork-ān) m. From *marc* 'a steed'. In the early period this name is more frequently found in the south of Ireland. Marcán mac Cennétig (†1010) was brother of Brian Boru and was abbot of the monasteries of Killaloe, Tomgraney and Emly. There is a St Marcán of Clonenagh whose feast-day is 21 October.

MARGO, MARGA (mor-ga) f. A name of uncertain origin. Margo from the fairy-mound was mother of the beautiful Étaín.

*MÁRGRÉG, MÁIRGRÉG, MÁIRGRÉC: MÁIRGHRÉAD, MÁIRÉAD (mār'-ēd) f. This is a borrowing of the Latin *margarita*, itself derived from a Greek word meaning 'pearl'. The name became popular in England and Scotland because of St Margaret, wife of Malcolm III of Scotland, who died in 1093. It became relatively popular in Ireland after the fourteenth century. The modern Irish forms *Peig* and *Peigí* are derived from English rhyming forms of *Meg* and *Meggie*, themselves pet-forms of Margaret. Among the forms now common in Ireland as well as in England are *Maggie*, *Mag*, *Madge*, *Maisie* and *Meg*.

*MARTAN (mort-an) m. This name became popular among clerics in early Ireland as a result of widespread devotion to St Martin of Tours whose cult was well-known in Ireland. Among the clerics who bore the name were Martan, bishop of Clonkeen, who died in 837 and Martan, abbot of Clonmacnoise and Devenish, who died in 869. The form *Máirtín*, now the current form in Irish, is a later borrowing.

*MARTHA f. This biblical name was borrowed in Ireland as early as the eighth century when it was borne by an abbess of Kildare who died in 758.

MATHA (mo-ha) m. This early Irish name may be a shortened form of the name of an early Celtic deity. In Irish legend, Matha mac Úmóir is one of the druids of the Tuatha Dé Danann. It has on occasion been used as an equivalent of the biblical name *Matthew*.

MATHGAMAIN, MATHGHAMHAIN: MATHÚIN (mo-hūn') m, 'bear-calf'. Mathgamain was brother of Brian Boru and king of Cashel. Another Mathgamain, who died in 1019, was claimant to the kingship of Munster. The name became relatively popular in later medieval Ireland among the O Briens, O Connors, O Farrells and others. In the fourteenth century it was latinised *Matheus* and as early as the seventeenth century it was equated with the biblical *Matthew*. It could more properly be anglicised *Mahon*. From it derive the modern surnames O Mahoney and Mac Mahon.

MECHAR: MEACHAR (m'a-char) m, 'fine, majestic'. This name occurs principally in Munster. Mechar mac Cáellaide was ancestor of the O Meaghers of Éile. There is also an early saint of the name.

MEDB: MEADHBH, MEADHBHA, MÉABH (mév) m and f, 'intoxicating, she who makes men drunk'. This is primarily a female name, being one of the twenty most popular names in later medieval Ireland, but it occurs as a male name in the very early period. The best-known bearer of this name is undoubtedly Medb Lethderg, the goddess of the sovereignty of Tara and wife of the legendary Art mac Cuinn. Medb, the headstrong queen of Connacht in *Táin Bó Cuailgne* is probably a later literary re-incarnation of her. In the christian tradition, one Medb of the Ciarraige was the mother of St Lugaid mac Luchta. The name was in use especially in the north of Ireland until the late nineteenth century where it is now obsolete and replaced by the English 'translations' *Madge*, *Magey* and *Marjory*. It has also been 'translated' *Maud*, *Mabbina*, *Mab*, *Mabbie* and *Mabel*. A more acceptable anglicisation, *Maeve* or *Meave*, is now very popular. There is also an Irish diminutive form *Meidhbhín*.

135

MEL (mel) m. St Mel is bishop and patron of Ardagh. His feast-day is 6 February. In hagiographical legend his mother was Darerca, sister of St Patrick.

MELL, MELLA: MEALL, MEALLA (m'al, m'al-a) f. This name is derived from an early word for 'lightning'. In Irish legend Mell, sister of St Cáemgen (Kevin), was mother of seven saints. Mella was the name of the mother of St Manchán of Lemanaghan.

MELLÁN: MEALLÁN (m'al-án) m. For derivation, see *Mell*. There are three early Irish saints of this name: St Mellán of Cell Rois whose feast-day is 28 January; St Mellán of Lough Corrib whose feast-day is 7 February; and St Mellán of Loughbrickland whose feast-day is 26 October. From this name derives the modern surname Ó Mealláin (O Mallin, Mallon).

MENMA: MEANMA (m'an-ma) m, 'high spirit, courage'. This name is peculiar to the Mac Namaras and to the Cianachta who claimed relationship with them.

MIADACH: MIADHACH, MIACH (mīach) m and f, 'honourable, proud'. According to the Finn-ballads Miadach is one of the ladies of the *fianna*. The name also occurs as a male name.

*MÍCHÉL: MÍCHEÁL m. A borrowing of the biblical name *Michael*. It was rare in Ireland until relatively recent times but it is now very popular. Mícheál is still the normal form in the Irish of Waterford and the diminutive form *Michealtaigh* was once common in Derry and Omeath.

MIDABAIR: MIODHABHAIR, MÍODHÚIR (m'ī-ūr') f. Midabair was sister of St Berach and was 'a holy and honourable virgin' who founded a church at Bumlin, Co Roscommon.

MIDIR (m'id'-ir') m. O Rahilly maintains that this name is connected with the verb *midiur* 'I judge' and sees Midir as meaning 'lord of the Otherworld' but other scholars consider the name a borrowing from some other language unknown to us. In Irish mythology, Midir is a magic personage, son of In Dagda ('the Good God') and lover of the beautiful Étaín.

MIDNAT: MIODHNAIT, MÍONAIT (m'ī-nit') f. There are two saints of this name: St Midnat whose feast-day is 18 November and St Midnat of Killucan, in Westmeath, whose feast-day is 4 August.

MÍNCHLOTH (m'īn'-chlō) f. Meaning, perhaps, 'of gentle reputation'. Míncloth was the mother of St Columb of Terryglass.

MO BÍ: MOIBHÍ (mu-v'ī) m. Mo Bí is a pet-form both of *Berchán* and *Brénainn* (which see). The best-known bearer of this name is St Mo Bí of Glasnevin whose feast-day is 12 October.

MO CHÁEMMÓC: MOCHAOMHÓG (mu-chēv-ōg) m. Mo Chaemóc is a pet-form of *Cáemgen* and *Cáemán* (which see) and according to an early text there are twenty-one Irish saints who bore the name. Perhaps the best-known of these is Mo Cháemóc of Leamakevoge near Two-Mile Borris, Co Tipperary, whose feast-day is 13 March.

MO CHOLLA, MOCHOLLA (mu-chol-a) m. This is, perhaps, a pet-form of *Columb* (which see). There were thirteen Irish saints of the name.

MO CHONNA, MOCHONNA (mu-chun-a) m. According to an early text there were twenty-nine Irish saints of this name. Among these are St Mo Chonna of the area near Elphin whose feast-day is 8 March and St Mo Chonna of Mayo whose feast-day is 27 March.

MO CHUA, MOCHUA (mu-ch-ua) m. Mo Chua is a pet-form of *Crónán* (which see). According to an early text there were fifty-nine saints of this name. Among the better known of these are St Mo Chua of Clondalkin whose feast-day is 6 August; St Mo Chua mac Lonáin of Timahoe whose feast-day is 24 December; and St Mo Chua of Balla whose feast-day is 30 March.

MO CHUMMA: MOCHUMA (mu-chum-a) m. Mo Chumma is generally a pet-form of *Colmán* (which see) and an old text says that there are thirty-three saints of the name. One of these is St Mo Chumma of Druim Ailche (Drumully, Co

Fermanagh) whose feast-day is 4 January.

MO CHUTU: MOCHUDA (mu-chud-a) m. Mo Chutu is a pet-form of *Carthach* (which see). St Mo Chutu was founder of Lismore and his feast-day is 14 May. This name has been anglicised *Carthage*.

MO LAISSE, MOLAISSE (mu-los'-e) m. This is a pet-form of *Laisrén* (which see). Traditionally there are forty-six saints of this name. The best-known of them are St Mo Laisse of Devenish whose feast-day is 12 September; St Mo Laisse of Kilmolash near Clonmel whose feast-day is 17 January; and St Mo Laisse of Leighlin whose feast-day is 15 April. This name was used as a personal name until recently among the O Meehans of Leitrim, by whom it was anglicised *Lazarus*.

MO LUA, MOLUA (mu-lūa) m. Mo Lua is a pet-form of *Lugaid* (which see). According to Irish tradition there were thirty-eight saints of the name. Perhaps the best-known of these is St Mo Lua moccu Óche of Clonfertmulloe whose feast-day is 4 August.

MOCHTA (much-ta) m. Meaning, possibly, 'great'. The best-known bearer of this name is St Mochta of Louth whose feast-day is 24 March.

MÓIRNE (mōr'-n'e) f. Probably a derivative of *Mór* (which see) which was in use in Omeath down to the end of the nineteenth century. It was anglicised *Maud* and *Maria*.

MONCHA (mun-cha) f. This name derives from **Monapiā* which was probably the name of a Celtic tribal goddess. In Irish legend, Moncha is wife of Eógan Mór, legendary ancestor of the Eóganacht. This name has been equated with *Monica*, with which it has no connection.

MONGÁN (mung-ān) m. From *mong* 'a head of long and abundant hair'. Mongán mac Fiachnai was an early literary hero of Dál nAraide. From Mongán derives the modern surname Ó Mongáin (O Mangan).

MONGFIND: MOINGFHIONN, MOINGIONN (mong'-in) m and f, 'fair-haired'. In Irish story, Mongfind was daughter of Feradach Finn, king of the Picts. Another Mongfind was daughter of Fidach and sister of Crimthann Már, legendary king of Ireland and Scotland. Mongfind was also the name of the mother of St Iarlaithe (Jarlath) of Tuam. Mongfind occurs as a man's name in some very early pedigrees but it is not common.

MÓR (mōr) f, 'tall, great'. Mór is by far the most popular female name in use in later medieval Ireland. According to tradition, Mór of the Cenél Conaill was mother of St Colmán Ela. In the tenth century, two queens of Ireland bore the name and Mór, daughter of Domnall mac Lochlainn, king of the North, was wife of Tairdelbach Ua Conchobair (Turlough O Connor), king of Ireland. Mór was also the name of the sister of St Laurence (Lorcán) O Toole. The name was equally popular in the later period. Mór, daughter of Mac Cába, who died in 1527 is described in the annals as 'the nurse of the learned and the destitute of Ireland' and Mór, daughter of O Carroll, who died in 1548, was wife of the earl of Desmond. This early name was latinised as *Morina* and anglicised *Martha* and *Agnes* but in the nineteenth century it was almost invariably anglicised *Mary* and thus accounts for the present popularity of Mary among Irish women. There is a diminutive form *Móirín* which has been anglicised *Moreen*.

MORAND: MORANN (mur-an) m. Morand was a legendary judge of the Irish who never gave a false judgment. According to the Finn-ballads, there were ten warriors of the name in the *fianna*. The name was also used by Christian clerics such as Morann mac Indrechtaig, abbot of Clogher, who died in 842 and Morand, bishop of Nendrum, who died in 684.

MUADÁN: MUADHÁN (mū-ān) m. Derived from *muad* 'noble, good'. There are two saints of this name: St Muadán of Kilmodan, Co Longford, whose feast-day is 6 March and St Muadán of Errigal, Co Monaghan, whose feast-day is 30 August.

MUADNAT: MUADHNAIT (mūa-nit') f, feminine form of *Muadán* (which see). St Muadnat is a virgin saint of Drumcliffe, Co Sligo, whose feast-day is 6 January. In the legends of the saints she is said to be a sister of the famous St Mo Laisse of Devenish. *Monat* and *Mona* have been used as anglicisations of this name.

MUGAIN: MUGHAIN (mūn') f. Mugain, in Irish mythology, appears to be one of the territorial goddesses of the south of Ireland. In the Christian tradition, Mugain and her sister Feidelm, two daughters of Ailill mac Dúnlaing, king of Leinster, are the patronesses of the parish of Tallaght, Co Dublin. Their feast-day is 9 December. There is another St Mugain, virgin of Clonburren, whose feast-day is 15 December. It is possible that the word *mugain* originally meant 'a young (unmarried) girl'.

MUGRÓN: MUGHRÓN (mū-rōn) m. Meaning, perhaps, 'lad of the seals'. This name was very popular in early Irish society. Among its bearers were Mugrón, king of Connacht (†872); Mugrón, abbot of Iona (†981); and Mugrón Ua Morgair, chief scholar of Armagh (†1102).

MUIRECHT: MUIREACHT√ (mir'-acht) f. Muirecht was daughter of Echu and, in legend, wife of Láegaire mac Néill, king of Tara.

MUIRCHERTACH: MUIRCHEARTACH (mir'-art-ach) m, 'skilled in seacraft, mariner'. This was an extremely common name in early and medieval Ireland. Muirchertach mac Erca is one of the legendary high-kings. The name was borne by two of the kings of Ireland in the twelfth century: Muirchertach Ua Briain who died in 1119 and Muirchertach Mac Lochlainn who was slain in 1166. It was common among the O Briens, the O Connors of Offaly and, down to very recent times, among the Mac Loughlins, O Brollaghans (Bradleys) and other northern families. In the north, *Mreartach* was a common form while the form *Briartach* occurred in Connacht. At an early period the name was latinised *Mauricius*. It was generally anglicised *Mortimer*, *Murt*, *Murty*, *Monty* (in Kerry) and, perhaps on occasion, *Maurice*. The best anglicised form is *Murtaugh*. The common sixteenth-century form is *Moriartogh*.

MUIRECÁN: MUIREAGÁN (mir'-ag-ān) m. Perhaps a

diminutive of *muire* 'a lord'. This was a relatively popular early name and was borne by a number of Leinster kings.

MUIREDACH: MUIREADHACH, MUIRÍOCH (mir'-īch) m. Perhaps from *muiredach* 'a lord, a master'. This was one of the more popular early names. Muiredach Tírech was one of the remote legendary ancestors of the Uí Néill. Muiredach Mál, in legendary history, is one of the ancestors of the Connachtmen while Muiredach Muillethan (†702) was king of Connacht and ancestor of the O Connor kings of Connacht. Muiredach mac Carthaig is ancestor of the Mac Carthys. According to the Finn-ballads, there are ten of the name in the *fianna*. St Muiredach, whose feast-day is 12 August, is patron of the diocese of Killala. The name could be anglicised *Murry* or *Murray*.

MUIRENN: MUIREANN (mir'-an) f. Meaning, perhaps, 'sea-white, sea-fair'. This was an extremely popular name in the early period. In the Finn-tales, Muirenn is daughter of Derg and foster-mother of the hero, Cáel. Muirenn is also the name of Oisín's wife. Another Muirenn was wife of Rogallach, ancestor of the kings of Connacht, and afterwards wife of the high-king Diarmait mac Aeda Sláine. The name was borne by four abbesses of Kildare among whom was Muirenn, sister of Fínnechta, king of Leinster who died in 831. An Irish princess, Muirenn, is mentioned in the Icelandic *Landnámabok* in the form *Myrun*. *Marion* and *Madge* appear to have been used as translations of Muirenn.

MUIRGEN: MUIRGHEIN, MUIRÍN (mir'-īn') m and f, 'born of the sea'. This early name is borne by St Muirgen, abbot of Killeshin, whose feast-day is 27 January. As a female name, its most famous bearer is the half-pagan, half-christian Muirgen, also known as Lí Ban ('Beauty of Women'). According to story, she lived for three hundred years in the waters of Lough Neagh until she was captured by Béoán, St Comgall's fisherman. Comgall baptised her, she told him her adventures, died and went to heaven.

MUIRGEL: MUIRGHEAL, MUIRÍOL (mir'-īl) f, 'sea-bright, sea-white'. Muirgel was the name of the wife of the king of Leinster who died in 854. Another Muirgel, daughter of the high-king, Máel Sechnaill I, died at an advanced age in Clonmacnoise in 928. Muirgel was also the name of one of the wives of the famous Leinster king, Cellach Cualann. It has been suggested that the popular name *Muriel* is derived from Muirgel. Muirgel also occurs as a man's name in the early pedigrees.

MUIRGIUS: MUIRGHEAS, MUIRÍOS (mir'-īs) m, 'sea-strength'.   This name was especially favoured by the noble families of Connacht both in the earlier and later medieval period. Muirgius mac Tomaltaig, king of Connacht, died in 815 while Muirgius mac Conchobair, claimant to the king-ship of Connacht, died in 988. In the later medieval period, Muirgius was a favoured name among the Mac Donaghs, Mac Dermotts and other Connacht families. It became *Maurice*, it appears, among the O Connells of Kerry and other families.

MUIRNE (mir'-n'e) f. Meaning, perhaps, 'high-spirited, festive'.   In Irish story, Muirne MunchÁem is mother of Finn mac Cumaill.

MUNNU: MUNA (mun-a) m, a pet-form of *Fintan* (which see).   St Munnu was abbot of Clonenagh and his feast-day is 21 October.

MURA (mur-a) m, a pet-form of *Murchad* (which see).   St Mura of the Cenél Eógain is founder and patron of Fahan in Inisowen. By misunderstanding, the name has come recently to be used as a female name.

MURCHAD: MURCHADH (mur-a-cha) m, 'sea-battler'. Murchad was one of the more popular early Irish names. Among its bearers were Murchad mac Briain, king of Leinster (†727), Murchad son of Brian Boru who was slain at Clontarf and Murchad mac Diarmada, ancestor of the Mac Murroughs of Leinster, who was slain in 1070. It was a favourite name among the O Briens, O Flahertys, O Connells, O Donovans and other families. *Brochadh* is a corrupt Connacht version of the name. It was latinised *Maurus*. It survived as a per-sonal name in the north down to the early nineteenth cen-tury while it was rendered *Morgan* among the O Connells,

142

O Donovans, Kavanaghs and other families. However, it retained its popularity among the O Briens in the form *Murrough* which is perhaps the best anglicisation.

MURCHÚ (mur-chū) m, 'hound of the sea'. A relatively uncommon early name. St Murchú, author of a life of St Patrick, was the most famous bearer of the name. His feast-day is 8 June.

n

NANNID: NINNIDH (n'in'-e') m. Nannid was legendary ancestor of the Cenél Conaill. There is also a St Nannid of Lough Erne whose feast-day is 18 June.

NÁRBFLAITH: NÁRBHFHLAITH, NÁRBHLA (nār-vla) f. Meaning, perhaps, 'noble princess'. Nárbflaith was daughter of the prince, Feradach mac Máel Dúin, and wife of Báethchellach, abbot of Trim (†756). The name could be anglicised *Narvla*.

NATH-Í: NAITHÍ (no-hī) m. This was a relatively common early name. Nath-í was grandson of Niall Naígiallach. Another Nath-í was grandson of the legendary king of Leinster, Énna Cenneselach. There are also three saints of the name. It has been anglicised *Nathy*.

NECHT: NEACHT (n'acht) f. Meaning, perhaps, 'pure'. This relatively rare name was borne by an early female saint.

NECHTAN: NEACHTAN (n'acht-an) m. This name is cognate with the name of the Roman god *Neptune* and means 'descendant of the waters'. In Irish legend, Nechtan is wife of Bóinn, the divinised Boyne. Among the saints of the name are St Nechtan of Killanny near Dundalk, whose feast-day is 2 May and St Nechtan of Dungiven, whose feast-day is 8 January. In the later middle ages, Nechtan was a favourite name among the O Donnells of Tír Chonaill. From this name derives the modern surname Ó Neachtain (O Naghten, Naughton, Norton).

NÉDE: NÉIDHE (n'ē) m. This is a very rare name of uncertain meaning. Néde mac Adna was one of the legendary judges of the Irish. In the later middle ages, this archaic name was affected by the learned family of Ó Maolchonaire (O Mulconry, Conry).

NÉM: NÉAMH (n'ēv) m and f. Perhaps identical with *Niam* (which see) and meaning 'sheen, brightness'. St Ném was a bishop from Kells whose feast-day is 18 February. In saga, Ném is daughter of the Ulster hero, Celtchar mac Uithechair and wife of the great warrior, Conganchnes mac Dedaid.

NEMON: NEAMHAIN (n'av-in') f, 'battle-fury, warlike frenzy'. This is the name of an ancient war-goddess of the Irish.

NÉMNACH: NÉAMHNACH (n'ēv-nach) f. For derivation, see *Ném*. In the legends of the saints, Némnach was mother of St Moling of Lúachair.

NESS: NEAS, NEASSA (n'as, n'as-a) f. In the sagas, Ness is daughter of Echu Sálbuide and mother of Conchobar mac Nessa, king of Ulster. In the legends of the saints, Ness, daughter of Fáelán, is mother of St Mo Cháemmoc and sister of St Íte.

NESSÁN: NEASÁN (n'as-ān) m. There are some five saints of this name, one of them being a friend of St Finnbarr of Cork. The best-known of them is St Nessán, deacon of Mungairit (Mungret), whose feast-day is 25 July. *Nessan* is the form now in use in English.

NIALL (n'íal) m. The derivation of this name is uncertain. O Rahilly felt that it was connected with *nél* 'a cloud' while Pokorny derives it from an ancient root meaning 'passionate, vehement'. The name was made famous by Niall Naígiallach ('of the Nine Hostages'), ancestor of the Uí Néill. Among other famous bearers of this name were the high-kings Niall Frassach (†778), Niall Caille (†846) and Niall Glúndub (†919). It was a favourite name among the O Neills, O Donnells, O Boyles, O Dohertys, O Higgins and other families and retained its popularity, in the form *Néill*, among the O Donnells, O Quinns, O Kellys and other northern families down to the end of the nineteenth century. It was latinised *Nicholas* (as early as the fifteenth century) and *Nigellus*.

NIALLÁN (n'ïal-ān) m, a diminutive of *Niall* (which see). From this name derives the modern surname Ó Nialláin (O Neylan, Neilan, Nealon).

NIAM: NIAMH (n'ïav) f, 'brightness, radiance, lustre'. Originally a goddess-name, this may have been the early name of the Munster Blackwater. In saga, Niam was one of the wives of the Ulster warrior, Conall Cearnach and was loved by Cúchulainn. Another Niam was daughter of Óengus Tírech, legendary king of Munster. She eloped with Oisín and spent six weeks hunting with him in Ulster. But the lovers were pursued by her father and the men of Munster and she died of fear. According to another story Niam was daughter of Áed Donn, king of Ulster, and it was over her that Oisín fought his first battle. According to the later Finn-tales, Niamh Chinn Óir was the beautiful fairy woman who loved Oisín and bore him off to the Land of Promise.

*NIOCLÁS, NICOL, m. This is the name of St Nicholas, bishop of Myra, patron of children and sailors. It became a favourite name in England in the twelfth century and was brought into Ireland by the Anglo-Normans. There is a diminutive form *Coilín* (which see). *Nicolás* could stand for *Niall* (which see) in the middle ages.

*NÓE m. This is the biblical *Noah* which was borrowed by some early medieval Irish clerics. There is a St Nóe of Finglas whose feast-day is 27 January. The name was not used outside ecclesiastical circles.

NOÍSE: NAOISE (nīs'-e) m. In the sagas, Noíse mac Uislenn is the tragic lover of the beautiful Deirdre. It was anglicised *Nyce* but it became *Noah* among the O Duigenans.

NUADU: NUADHA (nūa) m. In O Rahilly's opinion, Nuadu means 'the cloud-maker' and he is ultimately the ancestor-deity and lord of the Otherworld. Other scholars have suggested that Nuadu is the fisher-god. In the early historical tracts, Nuadu is a legendary hero and remote ancestor of many noble families. Nuadu Necht, for example, is considered to be the legendary ancestor of the Leinstermen. Despite its pagan associations, this name was borne by a number of saints and clerics. These are two saints of the name: St Nuadu the anchorite whose feast-day is 3 October and St Nuadu of Clones whose feast-day is 1 December. Among the clerics who bore the name are Nuadu, abbot of Armagh (†811) and Nuadu, abbot of Tuam (†781).

ÓCÁN: ÓGÁN (ōg-ān) m, 'youth, lad'. From this name derives the modern surname Ó hÓgáin (O Hogan, Hagan).

ODAR: ODHAR (ōr) m. This name may mean 'dark, sallow, grey-brown', but it is possible that here we have the ancient name of the otter used as a personal name. This is a relatively rare early name. Among its bearers is Odar mac Muiredaig, abbot of Lusk, who died in 1055.

ODARNAT: ODHARNAIT, ÓRNAIT (ōr-nit′) f. This is the female form of *Odrán* (which see) and is itself derived from *Odar* (which see). St Odarnat is a virgin saint whose feast-day is 13 November. The name could be anglicised *Ornat* or *Orna*.

ODRÁN: ODHRÁN, ÓRÁN (ōr-ān) m. For derivation, see *Odar*. According to an early text there were seventeen saints of this name. Among these are St Odrán of Latteragh in Ormond whose feast-day is 2 October; the saintly bishop Odrán whose feast-day is 8 May; and St Odrán who, according to tradition, was brother of St Ciarán of Clonmacnoise and whose feast-day is 16 May. This name could be anglicised *Oran*.

ÓENGUS: ÁENGUS, AONGHUS (ēn-īs) m. Óengus is the young god of Irish tradition and it is a name borne by many legendary heroes. Óengus Tírech is one of the legendary ancestors of the O Briens, Mac Namaras and related families while Óengus mac Natfraích is one of the early kings of Càshel. Among the Déisi, Óengus Gaí Buaibthech is perhaps

148

the greatest of their early heroes. There are five christian saints of the name among whom is Óengus Céile Dé whose feast-day is 11 March. Óengus mac Óengusa, who died in 932, is described in the annals as chief poet of Ireland. Óengus was a favourite name among the O Dalys, Mac Donnells and other families. The form *Naos* was formerly common in Omeath, Derry and Inishowen. The name Óengus survived among the Mac Donnells, Mac Alisters and Mac Cormacks of Antrim down to the end of the last century. It was generally anglicised as *Aeneas* and *Eenis* but was sometimes rendered *Niece*, *Neese*, *Niece* and, on occasion, *Nicholas*. *Enos* still occurs among a number of Munster families including the Foleys. *Angus* is the anglicised form in use in Scotland.

ÓENU: AONA (ēn-a) m, a pet-form of *Óengus* (which see). The best-known bearer of this name is St Óenu moccu Loígse, abbot of Clonmacnoise and successor of St Ciarán, whose feast-day is 20 January.

ÓENUCÁN: AONAGÁN (ēn-ag-ān) m, a diminutive form of *Óenu* (which see). Óenucán mac Ruadrach was an abbot of Lusk who died in 881. The name is relatively rare.

OILLÉOC: OILLEÓG (il'-ōg) m. Probably a diminutive of *Ailill* (which see). There is a St Oilléoc whose feast-day is 24 July.

OISSÍNE, OISSÉNE: OISÍN (us'-īn') m, a diminutive of *oss* 'a deer'. The best-known bearer of this name is Oissíne, son of Finn mac Cumaill, one of the great heroes of the Finn cycle. There were two saints of the name: St Oissíne whose feast-day is 1 May and St Oissíne of Clonmore, Co Louth, whose feast-day is 1 January. There was also an Oisséne, abbot of Clonmacnoise, who died in 706. This name has been anglicised *Ossian*.

OLCÁN (ulk-ān) m, 'a wolf'. This is a relatively rare early name.

ÓLCHOBAR: OLCHOBHAR (ōl-chūr) m, 'lover of drink'. This name is practically confined to Munster in the early period. Among its bearers were Ólchobar, abbot of Clonfert (†802), Ólchobar, abbot of Ros Ailithir (†933) and, perhaps the best-known of all, Ólchobar mac Cináeda, abbot of Emly and king of Munster, who died in 851. This name became obsolete at an early period.

*OLIBHÉAR m.   This is a borrowing of *Oliver*, a favourite medieval name. It was moderately common in England in the middle ages and was brought thence to Ireland where it was relatively common among the Geraldines and the Burkes in the sixteenth century. It became less common probably due to its association with Oliver Cromwell.

ONCHÚ (un-chū) m, 'fierce hound'.   Among the bearers of this name are St Onchú of Clonmore, Co Carlow, who is said to have collected the relics of the saints of Ireland and St Onchú of Dál Cais whose feast-day is 9 July.

*ONÓRA f.   This is a borrowing of the common Anglo-Norman name *Honora* which may be derived from Latin *honor* 'reputation, beauty'. *Annora* is the form commonly in use in England from the twelfth to the fourteenth century and the Irish form is a reflection of this. *Nóra*, *Nóirín* and *Nóinín* are now popular Irish forms. In Ulster, the accent shifted to the first syllable and the name became *Hannah* in Derry, and *Honor* in Omeath. Among the forms now in use in Ireland are *Honor*, *Nora*, *Noreen*, *Honora*, *Hanorah*, *Nonie*, *Nanno* and *Daisey*.

ÓRLAITH: ÓRLA (ōr-la) f, 'golden sovereignty, princess'. This was perhaps the fourth most popular name in twelfth-century Ireland. It was borne by both a sister and a niece of Brian Boru. Órlaith, daughter of Dermot Mac Murrough, was mother of Domnall Mór O Brien, king of Thomond. Tigernán O Rourke, king of Breifne, had a daughter Órlaith. However, it seems to have declined in popularity in the later middle ages.

ÓRNAT: ÓRNAIT (ōr-nit') f.   Among the bearers of this name were Órnat, wife of Guaire, king of Connacht, and Órnat, daughter of Cúán, king of Munster (†641).

ORTHANACH (ur-han-ach) m, 'potent in prayers (charms)'. Among the bearers of this name are Orthanach, bishop of Kildare (†840), who wrote a long poem on the glories of

150

Kildare and Orthanach, abbot of Roscrea, who died in 952.

OSCAR: OSGAR (usk-ar) m. According to Pokorny, this name means 'deer-lover'. The most famous bearer of the name is Oscar, grand-son of Finn mac Cumaill, one of the great warriors of the Finn cycle. This name also occurs among the early ancestors of the Corcu Modruad (O Connors and Mac Loughlins of Clare). It also occurs amongst the Maguires in the fourteenth century.

OSCHÚ (us-chū) m, 'deer-hound'. A relatively rare early name which occurs amongst the Dál nAraide and the Déisi.

OSSÁN: OSÁN (us-án) m, diminutive of *oss* 'a deer'. A very early and relatively rare name. There is a St Ossán of Trim whose feast-day is 17 February.

OSSNAT: OSNAIT (us-nit') f, feminine form of *Ossán* (which see). There are two saints of this name: St Ossnat whose feast-day is 10 November and St Ossnat, reputed to have been a sister of the famous St Mo Laisse of Devenish, whose feast-day is 6 January.

p

*PARTHALÁN m. This is a borrowing of Latin *Bartho-lomaeus*. Among the forms in use are *Parthalán*, *Pártlán*, *Párthlán*, *Partnán* and *Beartlaoi*. It was anglicised *Berkley* and *Barclay* in Derry, *Barkley* in Omeath. *Bartley* and *Batt* are now common forms in Ireland.

*PÁTRAIC: PÁDRAIG. This is a borrowing of Latin *Patricius* 'a patrician'. The early Irish, out of respect for St Patrick, did not use the name itself but such forms as *Gilla Pátraic* 'servant of St Patrick' and *Máel Pátraic* 'devotee of St Patrick'. Patrick came into use as a personal name among the colonists in Ireland before it became common among the native Irish. When used by the Anglo-Normans it was rendered *Pádraigín* by the Irish. Writing in 1834, O Donovan declared: 'I do not believe that Patrick as the name of a man is a hundred and fifty years in use.' At present, Patrick is the fourth most popular name in Ireland and occurs in a bewildering variety of forms in Irish and English. Among the Irish forms are *Pádhraic*, *Páraic*, *Padhra*, *Páid*, *Páidí*, *Páidín*, *Paidí*, *Paití* and *Parra*. The female form, *Patricia*, seems to have begun in Scotland in the eighteenth century but it became popular only in the present century. Its Irish translation, *Pádraigín*, is a modern invention. *Paitín*, which may be a derivative of *Pátraic*, is to be found amongst the learned family of Ó Maolchonaire as early as the thirteenth century.

*PETRÁN: PEADRÁN m. This name is a diminutive of *Petrus*. It was borrowed by Irish clerics as early as the seventh century but never achieved any popularity.

*PEADAR m. A borrowing of the name *Peter*. *Peadar* is the modern form, *Piaras* being the medieval form.

*PIARAS m. This is a borrowing of *Piers*, the Anglo-Norman French form of *Peter*, introduced into Ireland by the Anglo-Norman settlers. The diminutive form *Piarag* occurs in the fourteenth century. From this derives the surname *Mac Phiaraig* (Feerick).

*PILIB m. This is a borrowing of the Greek name *Phillip* (horse-lover) which was extremely popular in medieval England and which was brought into Ireland by the Anglo-Norman settlers. It became extremely popular among some Irish families, the Maguires in particular. The form *Philpog* is found among the Tyrrells and Daltons of Westmeath down to the seventeenth century.

*PÓL m. This is a borrowing of the name of St Paul, apostle of the Gentiles. It was used in various forms by the early Irish clergy but it was rare here—as it was in Anglo-Saxon England. It has become relatively common in Ireland only in recent times.

*PROINNSIAS m. This is a borrowing of the name of St Francis of Assisi (†1226). The earliest English examples of this name date from the fifteenth century and it probably passed from England to Ireland at a later period. *Preanndaigh*, a pet-form, was in use in Omeath down to the beginning of this century.

R

*RAGNALL: RAGHNALL (rei-nal) m. A borrowing from the Old Norse. This was the name of many Vikings who had settled in Ireland. One Ragnall mac Amlaíb was slain at the battle of Tara in 980. Ragnall mac Ímair, king of Waterford, died in 1018. It was soon borrowed by the Irish and became relatively popular. Ragnall Ua Dálaig was principal poet of Desmond and died in 1161. In the later middle ages the name was favoured by the Meic Branáin of Connacht and by the Meic Ragnaill (now usually Reynolds) of Muinter Eolais. Among the Mac Donnells of Antrim it was particularly favoured in the form *Randal*—they pronounced it *Rannal*.

*RAGNAILT: RAGHNAILT (rein-ilt') f, a feminine form of *Ragnall* (which see). Raghnailt became a favourite woman's name in later medieval Ireland. Ragnailt, daughter of Ó Fócarta, was mother of Domnall Mór O Brien, King of Thomond. Áed Ua Conchobair, king of Connacht (†1393), had a daughter Ragnailt. It was occasionally latinised as *Regina*.

RAICHBE: RAICHBHE (ra-v'e) f. In Irish hagiographical legend Raichbe was the virgin sister of St Ciarán of Clonmacnoise.

RATHNAT: RATHNAIT (roh-nit') f. St Rathnat is the patroness of Kilraghts, Co Antrim, and her feast-day is 5 August.

REBACHÁN: REABHACHÁN (row-chan) m, 'skilled in feats of valour, nimble'. The best-known bearer of this

154

somewhat rare name was Rebachán mac Mothlai, king of
Dál Cais and abbot of Tuaim Gréne (Tomgraney), who
died in 934.

RECHTABRA: REACHTABHRA, REACHTÚRA (r'acht-
ūr-a) m. In the early period this name was borne by Rechtabra,
son of Flann Feórna, a prince of the Ciarraige who died in
741; Rechtabra, king of Corcu Baiscind and ancestor of the
O Linnanes and the Baskins, who died in 844; and Rechtabra,
abbot of Clonfert, who died in 850.

*RÉMANN: RÉAMONN (r'ē-mun) m. A borrowed name from
Old German *ragan* 'counsel' and *mund* 'protection'. It was
introduced into England by the Normans and brought thence
to Ireland by the Anglo-Norman settlers. It became quite
popular in later medieval Ireland and until the nineteenth
century it was popular among the O Hanlons, Mac Canns,
Mac Ardles, Mackens and other northern families. It was
generally anglicised *Redmond*.

RIAGUIL: RIAGHAIL (r'īl') m. This is an early ecclesiastical
name and there are three saintly bearers of it: St Riaguil mac
Búachalla whose feast-day is 13 April; St Riaguil of Bangor
whose feast-day is 11 June; and St Riaguil, abbot of Muccinis
on Lough Derg, whose feast-day is 16 October.

RÍAN: RIAN (r'īan) m. Most likely a diminutive of *rí* a 'king'.
There is a St Rían whose feast-day is 23 April. From this
name derives the modern surname Ó Riain (O Ryan).

*RICARD: RIOCARD (r'i-kard) m. A borrowing of Old
German *Ricohard* from *ric* 'ruler' and *heard* 'hard', its popularity in medieval England being due to importation from the
continent. *Richard* and *Ricard* were equally common in
medieval England and each was imported to Ireland giving
respectively *Risderd* and *Ricard* in Irish. *Risderd* is the
contemporary form in the Irish of Waterford. The form
Risderd seems to have been particularly favoured by the
Butlers in the later middle ages. *Risdeag* is a later medieval
diminutive.

RÍGÁN: RÍOGHÁN (r'ī-ān) m, a diminutive of *rí* 'a king'.
A relatively rare early name.

RÍGBARDDÁN: RÍOGHBHARDÁN, RÍORDÁN (r'īr-dān) m, 'royal poet'. This early name is found principally in Munster. Rígbarddán mac Con Coirne, king of the Éile, died in 1058. Rígbarddán mac Assída an early noble of the Eóganacht of Cashel, is ancestor of the Uí Rígbarddáin (O Riordans). The name could be anglicised *Riordan* or *Rearden*.

RÍGNACH: RÍOGHNACH, RÍONACH (r'īn-ach) f, 'queenly'. There are two saints of the name: St Rígnach whose feast-day is 18 December and St Rígnach, sister of St Finnén of Clonard, whose feast-day is 9 February. There was another Rígnach who, according to tradition, was the mother of the early warriors Conall and Eógan and thus ancestress of the O Neills, Mac Loughlins, O Donnells, O Gallaghers, O Gormleys and other northern families. This name has apparently been anglicised *Regina*.

RÍOMTHACH: RÍOMHTHACH, RÍOFACH (r'ī-fach) f. St Ríomthach was daughter of Lénine and is one of the patronesses of Killiney. Her feast-day is 6 February.

ROBARTACH: ROBHARTACH (rŏ-art-ach) m. Meaning, possibly, 'rushing, impetuous'. Robartach mac Máele hUidir, abbot of Aghaboe, died in 836. Another Robartach, anchorite of Clonmacnoise, died in 1007. From this name derives the modern surname Mac Robhartaigh (Mac Roarty, Groarty).

RODÁN (ru-dān) m. There is a St Rodán whose feast-day is 24 August.

ROGELLACH, ROGALLACH: RAGHALLACH (reil-ach) m. This is a relatively uncommon name. There was a Ragallach mac Uatach, king of Connacht, who died in 648. From this name derives the modern surname Ó Raghallaigh (O Reilly).

RÓINSECH, RÓNSECH: RÓINSEACH (rōn'-s'ach) f. Derived from *rón* 'a seal'. Róinsech was the name of the wife of an early king of Airgialla and there is also a St Róinsech.

*RÓIS, RÓISE, RÓS (rŏs', rŏs) f. This name appears to derive from the Old German *hros* 'horse' though at an early period it was identified with the flower of that name. It was brought into England by the Normans and reached Ireland much later. It was in use among the Uí Chatháin (O Kanes) of Ulster in the sixteenth century and was still common in Derry and Omeath, at the beginning of this century, among the O Kanes and the O Murrays. *Róisín* is a popular diminutive form.

RÓNÁN (rŏn-ān) m. Derived from *rón* 'a seal'. Rónán was a relatively popular name in early Ireland. According to ecclesiastical sources, there were ten saints of the name. Among these are St Rónán of Lough Derg whose feast-day is 13 January; St Rónán of Lismore (†763), whose feast-day is 9 February; St Rónán of Dromiskin, Co Louth, whose feast-day is 18 November; and St Rónán Finn (†664) of Magheralin whose feast-day is 22 May and who, according to story, cursed Suibne Gelt (Mad Sweeney) who went mad at the battle of Moira.

RÓNCHÚ (rŏn-chū) m, 'seal-hound'. A rare early name which occurs among the Dál Cais.

RÓNNAT: RÓNAIT, RÓNNAD (rŏn-it') f, the feminine form of *Rónán* (which see). Among the bearers of this name are Rónnat, daughter of Áed Sláne, the high-king, and Rónnat mother of St Adamnán.

ROSS, RUSS: ROSS, ROSA (rus) m. In the early period Ross was a relatively common name for legendary heroes and founders of dynasties. There is also a St Ross of Down. In the forms *Rossa* and *Rosa* it occurs in the fifteenth and six-teenth centuries among the Mac Mahons of Oriel, the O Farrells, the Magennises, the Mac Coughlins and the Maguires. At the beginning of this century Ross was still common as a man's name in southern Ulster and it also occurred in Inisowen.

RÚADACÁN: RÚADHAGÁN (rūa-gān) m. From *rúad* 'red-haired'. A relatively uncommon early Irish name.

RÚADÁN: RÚADHÁN (rūān) m. From *rúad* 'red-haired'. The most famous bearer of this name was St Rúadán, founder of the monastery of Lorrha, whose feast-day is 15 April. It is anglicised as *Rowan*.

RÚADNAT: RÚADHNAIT (rŭa-nit') f, female form of *Rúadán* (which see). In the legends of the saints St Rúadnat is sister of St Rúadán of Lorrha.

RUAIDRÍ: RUAIDHRÍ, RUAIRÍ (rŭa-r'ī) m, 'great king, red king'. Ruaidrí was a favourite name in medieval Ireland. Among its bearers were Ruaidrí na Saide Buide, king of Connacht, who died in 1118 and Ruaidrí Ua Conchobair (O Connor), king of Connacht and last high-king of Ireland, who died in 1198. Ruaidrí was especially favoured by the O Connors of Connacht throughout the middle ages. It was anglicised *Roderick* among the O Connors but among the O Shaughnessys, O Mores and other families it became *Roger*. In the north, Ruaidrí was much favoured by the O Donnells, McGinleys, Logues, Mulloys, O Dohertys, Mac Donnells and Mac Canns. Here it was generally anglicised *Roger*, *Roddy* and *Rhoddy*, though in the nineteenth century it was equated with *Richard*. The best anglicised form is *Rory*.

RUARCC: RUARC (rŭark) m. This name may contain the old word *arg* 'a hero, a champion'. From this rare early name derives the surname Ó Ruairc (O Rourke). There is also a diminutive form *Ruarcán*.

RUDRAIGE: RUDHRAIGHE, RUARAÍ, (rŭa-rī) m. In the earliest texts this name seems, in fact, to be a tribal name and it is, perhaps, possible that it became confused with *Ruaidrí*. The earliest bearer of the name is Rudraige, grandfather of the early Ulster hero Fergus. It became popular among the O Dohertys, O Donnells, O Mores and a number of other families in the later middle ages.

RUISSÍNE: RUISÍN (ris'-ĭn') m, a diminutive of *Ross* (which see). This rare early name was borne by an abbot of Cork who died in 686. There is also a St Ruissíne of Spike Island whose feast-day is 7 April.

RUMANN: RUMHANN (ruv-an) m. This rare early name was borne by a son of Conall Gulban, founder of Cenél Conaill. Its most famous bearer was undoubtedly Rumann mac Colmáin of Trim who died *c.* 747. An early Irish text says:

'There are three great poets of the world: Homer of the Greeks, Virgil of the Latins, and Rumann of the Irish.'

S

SADB: SABHBH (seiv) m and f. Said to mean 'sweet'. While frequent enough in the earliest periods, Sadb is the second most popular female name in later medieval Ireland. Sadb, daughter of Conn Cétchathach ('of the hundred battles'), was wife of the legendary Munster king Ailill Ólom and, in story at least, was ancestress of the noblest families in Munster. Sadb Sulbair ('of the pleasant speech') was daughter of Ailill and of Medb, queen of Connacht. Brian Boru had a daughter Sadb who died in 1048. Sadb, daughter of O Kennedy, was wife of Donnchad Cairbreach O Brien, king of Thomond. In the nineteenth century, this name was generally anglicised *Sally*, a pet-form of *Sarah*, with which it has no connection. In Omeath, Sadb became *Sarah* while in Derry it was generally turned into *Sophia*. It was also rendered *Sophy*, *Sabia* and *Sabina*. The best anglicised form is *Sive*. *Sabha* and *Sadhbha* are dialectal forms of the name.

SÁERBRETHACH: SAOIRBHREATHACH (sēr'-vr'a-hach) m, 'noble of judgment'. Among the bearers of this name were Sáerbrethach Ua Cellaig, abbot of Rahan, who died in 1136 and Sáerbrethach, abbot of Emly, who died in 1025. Carthach, son of Sáerbrethach, was ancestor of the Mac Carthys and this name became extremely common among the Mac Carthys at the end of the middle ages and in the translated form, *Justin*, still retains its popularity amongst them. It was particularly favoured by the Mac Egans in the later medieval period.

SÁERLAITH: SAORLAITH, SAORLA (sēr-la) f, 'noble

160

princess'. This early name was borne by the mother of Máel Brigte mac Dornáin, abbot of Armagh.

SAMRADÁN: SAMHRADHÁN, SAMHRÁN (sow-rān) m, 'a summery person'. This rare name was borne by Samradán ancestor of Meic Samradáin (Mac Governs, Magowran, Magaurans).

SAMTHANN: SAMHTHANN (sav-han) f. St Samthann was foundress and abbess of the monastery of Clonbroney, near Granard. She died in 739 and her feast-day is 19 December.

*SANCTÁN (sank-tān) m. A borrowing from the Latin *sanctus* 'a saint'. St Sanctán was a bishop associated with Bohernabreena, Co Dublin, whose feast-day is 9 May.

SÁRAIT: SARAID (sār-it) f. From *sár* 'best, noble'. In legend Sárait, daughter of Conn Cétchathach, is ancestress of the Múscraige (peoples of Muskerry) and of the kings of Scotland.

SÁRÁN (sār-ān) m. This name may be derived from *sár* 'best, noble' but there is a rare noun *sár* which means 'chief, ruler'. Sárán was an early king of Ulster. There are three saints of the name: St Sárán of Cluain Crema (Clooncraff) whose feast-day is 8 January; St Sárán of Tisaran, Co Offaly, whose feast-day is 20 January; and St Sárán of Great Island in Cork Harbour whose feast-day is 15 May.

SÁRNAT: SÁRNAIT (sār-nit') f. Like *Sárait* (with which it is sometimes confused) this name is a feminine form of *Sárán* (which see). There is a St Sárnat, associated with the midlands, whose feast-day is 9 November.

SCANDAL: SCANNAL (skon-al) m. This name may be associated with *scandal* 'quarrel, contention'. This relatively early name was borne by Fergus Scandal, an early king of Munster, and by Scandal, abbot of Aghaboe, who died in 780. From it derives the modern surname Ó Scannail (O Scannell).

SCANDLACH: SCANNLACH (skon-lach) f, feminine form of *Scandal* (which see). In the Finn-tales, Scandlach is wife

161

of Goll mac Mórna, the great enemy of Finn. There is a St Scandlach of the race of the Uí Néill whose feast-day is 10 December. The name seems to have become obsolete at an early period.

SCANDLÁN: SCANNLÁN (skon-lān) m, a diminutive of *Scandal* (which see). This was a relatively common name in early Ireland. Scandlán Mór mac Cind Faelad (†646) was an early king of Ossory. Scandlán mac Taidc, abbot of Killaloe, died in 991. From this name derives the modern surname Ó Scannláin (O Scanlon).

SCÁTHACH (skā-hach) f, 'shadowy, ghostly, frightening'. In the Ulster tales, Scáthach is the female warrior, clearly an Otherworld personage, who taught Cúchulainn the use of weapons. In the Finn-tales, Scáthach, daughter of Énna, lulls Finn to sleep with magic music in a fairy mound.

SCIATH (sk'-ia) f. Sciath, daughter of Mechar, was a saint of the Múscraige. Her feast-day is 6 September.

SCOITHÍNE: SCOITHÍN (sku-hīn') m. Derived from *scoth* 'bloom, blossom'. There was a Scoithíne, abbot of Durrow, who died in 950 but the best-known bearer of the name is St Scoithíne whose feast-day is 2 January and who was remarkable for his great, if unconventional, austerities.

SCOLAIGE: SCOLAIGHE, SCOLAÍ (skul-ī) m, 'scholar, schoolman'. This name originated in the monasteries but spread into secular society. From it derives the modern surname Ó Scolaí (O Scully).

SCOTH (sku) f, 'bloom, blossom'. There are two virgin saints of this name, one whose feast-day is 18 January and another whose feast-day is 16 July.

SCOTHNAT: SCOTHNAIT (sku-nit') f. From *scoth* 'a blossom, a bloom'. This name was borne by the saintly nun, Scothnat of Cluain Becc, who was a pupil of St Finnbarr of Cork.

SCOTHNIAM: SCOITHNIAMH (sku-n'iav) f. A compound of *scoth* 'a bloom, a blossom' and *niam* 'shining, lustrous'. Scothniam, daughter of Bodb Derg (son of the Dagda), lived in the magic caves of Cruachain and was the mistress of the warrior Caílte.

*SÉAFRAID, SÉAFRAIDH, SÉAFRA (s'ēf-ra) m. This is a gaelicisation of the name *Geoffrey*, which was common in England in the later middle ages and which was brought into Ireland by the Anglo-Normans. It became very common among the O Donoghues. *Séartha*, *Seáthra* and *Seathrún* are variant forms of the name in Irish.

*SÉAMUS, SÉAMAS (s'ēm-as) m. A borrowing through English and French of the Latin *Jacobus*. This name was common among the Anglo-Norman settlers in Ireland and was adopted by the native Irish. *Séamuisín*, *Síomaigh*, *Siomataigh* are Irish diminutives. *Hamish* seems to be a bastard Scottish form developed from the vocative while, in Ireland, *Shamus* is a phonetic rendering of the Irish form. The form *Siacas* (from French *Jacques*) occurs commonly in the thirteenth and fourteenth centuries.

*SEAAN: SEÁN (s'ān) m. This name is a borrowing through French *Jehan* of the Latin *Joannes*. This name did not become popular in western Europe until after the first crusades but it was relatively popular in England from the twelfth to the fifteenth centuries, after which it became very common. It was brought into Ireland by the Anglo-Norman settlers but it was soon adopted by the Irish. Among the variants of the name in use in the middle ages are *Seóan*, *Seóinín*, *Seónag* and *Seinicín*. In modern Irish, the normal form is *Seán* (with a diminutive *Seáinín*) but the forms *Seón*, *Seóinín* and *Seantaigh* occurred in Omeath as late as the beginning of this century. *Shane* is a phonetic rendering of Irish *Seán*. From this name derives the modern surname Mac Seáin (Mac Shane).

*SECHNALL: SEACHNALL, SEACHLANN (s'ach-lan) m. A borrowing from the name of *Secundinus*, an early missionary in Ireland, after whom Dunshaughlin is named. His feast-day is 27 November. From this name derives the much more common personal name *Máel Sechnaill* (which see).

SÉGÁN: SÉAGHÁN (s'ē-ān) m. Probably derived from *séig*

'a hawk'.   A rare early name.

SÉGDAE: SÉAGHDHA, SÉ (s'ē) m. This name may mean 'hawk-like, fine, goodly'.   A relatively rare early name from which derives the modern surname Ó Séaghdha (Shea). It could be anglicised *Shay*.

SÉGNAT: SÉAGHNAIT, SÉANAIT (s'ēn-it) f, female form of *Ségán* (which see).   Ségnat was the abbess whom St Abbán placed in charge of his foundations in Meath. There is a St Ségnat whose feast-day is 18 December.

SÉIGÍNE: SÉIGHÍN (s'ē-īn', s'ein) m and f. Derived from *séig* 'a hawk'.   Among the bearers of this early name are Séigíne, fifth abbot of Iona, who died in 652; St Séigíne of Kilshine, near Navan, whose feast-day is 21 January; and St Séigíne of Armagh whose feast-day is 24 May. It is said that the modern Munster surname Shine derives from this name.

SELBACH: SEALBHACH (s'al-vach) m, 'having great possessions, a land-owner'.   This name was borne by one of the early ancestors of the O Donoghues. It was also the name of an eighth century abbot of Cork. According to the Finn-tales, Diarmait úa Duibne had a son of this name. From this derives the modern surname Ó Sealbhaigh (O Shally, Shalloo, Shallow, Shalvey).

SENACH: SEANACH (s'an-ach) m. Derived from *sen* 'ancient, old'.   This was a very common early Irish name and was, according to O Rahilly, the name of a pagan Irish god. There is a St Senach of Lough Erne whose feast-day is 11 May.

SENÁN: SEANÁN (s'an-ān) m, a diminutive from *sen* 'ancient, old'.   This name occurs in the early period among certain peoples in Clare. There were many saints of the name but the best-known of them is St Senán of Inish Cathaig (Scattery Island) whose feast-day is 8 March. The name has been anglicised *Senan, Sinan, Sinon, Synan* and, it has been suggested, *Simon*.

SENCHÁN: SEANCHÁN (s'an-chān) m, a diminutive of *Senach* (which see).   Among the bearers of this early name were Senchán, abbot of Emly, who died in 781 and Senchán Torpéist, one of the most famous early Irish poets.

SERC: SEARC (s'ark) f, 'love, affection'.   This rare name was borne by an early saint of Meath.

SÉTACH: SÉADACH (s'ēd-ach) f, 'having rich possessions'. This uncommon name was borne by an eleventh-century princess, daughter of Ó Lorcáin.

SÉTNA: SÉADNA (s'ē-na) m.   According to O Rahilly, this is a god-name which originally meant 'traveller, wayfarer'. This is a relatively common early name borne by legendary kings and dynastic founders such as Sétna Sithbacc whom the Leinstermen regarded as a remote ancestor. According to a medieval text, there are thirteen saints of the name among whom is St Sétna of Armagh whose feast-day is 9 March. This name has been anglicised *Sidney*.

*SIBÁN: SIOBHÁN (s'iv-ān) f.   This is a borrowing of *Jehane* or *Jehanne*, a French feminine form of *John*, which came into favour in the twelfth century and was brought into Ireland by the Anglo-Normans. Among the bearers of the name was Sibán, daughter of the third earl of Desmond and wife of Tadg Mac Carthaig, 'the most celebrated wine-bibber of his age'. In the nineteenth century, Sibán became anglicised *Susan*, *Judith* and *Judy* in the north, *Johanna*, *Joan* and *Hannah* in the south and west. It was also rendered *Susanna*, *Julia*, *Jude* and *Nonie*. *Sinéad* and *Sineaid* are Irish forms of the French and English diminutives *Jonet*, *Janeta* and *Jennet*.

*SIBÉAL, ISIBÉAL (s'i-b'ēl) f.   Isabel, the medieval French form of *Elizabeth*, first appeared in England in the twelfth century and became extremely popular. It was brought to Ireland by the Anglo-Normans. In Derry, it disappeared in the end of the nineteenth century and was rendered *Bella*, *Anabel* and *Arabella*, while in Omeath it was re-translated *Elizabeth* and *Lizzie*. It is also rendered *Isabella*, *Sybil*, *Sibby*, *Eliza* and *Bessie*.

*SÍLE (s'īl-e) f.   Síle is a borrowing of the Latin name *Caecilia* and was brought into Ireland by the Anglo-Normans.

In the nineteenth century it was re-translated *Julia*, *Judy*, *Judith*, *Jennie*, *Selia*, *Celia*, *Sabina* and *Sally*. The anglicised forms *Sheila*, *Shiela*, *Sheela* and *Shelagh* are now widely used in England as independent names. In the sixteenth and seventeenth centuries it becomes *Giles* or *Cecily*.

SILLÁN: SIOLLÁN (s'ul-ān) m.   This early name was borne by a number of Irish saints: St Sillán of Kildalkey, near Trim, whose feast-day is 31 January; St Sillán, bishop of Glendalough, whose feast-day is 10 February; and St Sillán of Bangor who died in 612 and whose feast-day is 28 February.

SÍTAE: SÍODA (s'īd-a) m.   This name may be related to the Irish for 'silk' or may be a pet-form of a longer name. The name occurs among the Dál Cais and was particularly favoured by the Mac Namaras. It is latinised as *Jacobus* in the middle ages. It is still used among the MacNamaras in the form *Sheedy*.

SÍTHMAITH: SÍODHMHAITH, SÍOMHA (s'ī-va) f. Derived from *síth* 'peace'.   Síthmaith was abbess of Clonburren and died in 778. The name could be anglicised *Seeva*.

SLÉBÍNE: SLÉIBHÍN (sl'ēv-īn) m, 'a mountainy man'.   The most famous bearer of this name was St Slébíne (†758), abbot of Iona, whose feast-day is 2 March. From it is derived the modern surname Ó Sléibhín (O Slavin, Slevin).

SLÁINE (slan'-e) f.   This name was common among the O Briens and Mac Namaras in the later middle ages. The Latin form is *Slanina*.

SOCHLA (such-la) f, 'well-reputed, renowned'.   Sochla was the name of the mother of St Feichín and of the mother of St Molua.

*SOLAM: SOLAMH (sul-av) m.   This is an old borrowing of the biblical name *Solomon* particularly favoured by the learned families of Mac Namee and Mac Egan. It was used until the end of the last century by the Mac Namees of Omagh but has since been retranslated *Solomon*.

*SOMHAIRLE (sōr'l'e, sowr'l'e) m. This is a borrowing from Old Norse *Summarliethi* 'summer-farer, viking'.   This name was particularly favoured by the Mac Donnells but was in use among the O Gormleys and other northern families. In the north of Ireland, it was anglicised *Charles* and *Charlie* while in Scotland it became *Samuel*. *Sorley* is, perhaps, the best anglicisation.

SORCHA (sur-cha) f, 'bright, radiant'.   This was a relatively common name in medieval Ireland and remained in use down to the nineteenth century when it was generally anglicised as *Sarah* and *Sally*.

*STIAMNA: STIAMHNA (st'īav-na) m.   This is a borrowing of the biblical Stephen, a name made popular in England by the Normans and brought by them into Ireland. Other forms in Irish are *Steimhín*, *Stiabhna*, *Stiana*, *Sleimhne* (in the thirteenth century) and, latterly, *Stiofán*. From this derives the surname Mac Sleimhne (Sleyne, Slyney, Slyne).

SUAIBSECH: SUAIBHSEACH (sūav'-s'ach) f, 'gracious, kindly'.   Suaibsech was the name of the mother of Máel Ruba, abbot of Bangor and founder of Aporcrossan (†722). There is also a St Suaibsech whose feast-day is 9 January.

SUANACH (sūan-ach) f, 'drowsy'.   In the Finn poems Suanach is sister of Finn and mother of the warrior Fiachra.

SUIBNE: SUIBHNE (siv'-n'e, sī-n'e) m.   Suibne is a very popular early Irish name. Among the saints of the name are St Suibne of Skellig whose feast-day is 28 April and St Suibne of Iona whose feast-day is 11 January. Suibne mac Máele hUmai, who died in 682, is the earliest recorded abbot of Cork. The name was also borne by Suibne Menn, high-king, who died in 630. Perhaps the best-known bearer of the name is Suibne Gelt (Mad Sweeney) who was cursed by St Rónán, went mad at the battle of Moira, and spent the rest of his days wandering as a wild bird-man throughout the woods of Ireland. From this name derives the modern surname Mac Suibhne (Mac Sweeney). *Saibhne* appears to be an Omeath variant of the name. It was, on occasion, anglicised *Simon*.

ᴄ

TADC: TADHG (teig) m, 'a poet'. This name was relatively common in the early period and became extremely popular later. Brian Boru had a son, Tadc, who died in 1023. Among the kings of Connacht of the name are Tadc mac Cathail, who died in 925, and Tadc an Eich Gil ('of the bright steed'), who died in 1030. One of the greatest of the later bardic poets was Tadc Dall Ó hUiginn. In modern Irish Tadc, one of the commonest of names, is used as Jack is in English. *Tadhg an mhargaidh* or *Tadhg na sráide* means 'the man in the street'; *Tadhg an dá thaobh* means 'a double-dealer'; and *Tadhg na scuab* means 'the man in the moon'. In the nineteenth century it was generally anglicised *Thady* but it was also rendered *Thaddaeus*, *Theophilus* and *Theodosius*. In the north, it was generally anglicised *Teague*, a name now applied to all Catholics. *Timothy*, *Tim* and *Ted* are now the most commonly used equivalents. All these later substitutes are, of course, totally different names of biblical or classical origin. Timothy was already borrowed as *Tiamdae* in the Old Irish period.

TADGÁN: TADHGÁN (teig-ān) m, a diminutive of *Tadc* (which see). From this derives the modern surname Ó Tadhgáin (O Tagan, Teegan).

TAILECH: TUILEACH (tal'-ach) f. Meaning, perhaps, 'having a prominent forehead'. St Tailech was one of the three holy virgins of Uí Loscáin, an early Leinster tribe.

TAILEFHLAITH: TUILELAITH (til'-a-la) f. Meaning, perhaps, 'abundance of sovereignty, lady of abundance'.

Tailefhlaith was abbess of Clonguffin, Co Meath. She died in 782. There is a St Tailefhlaith who was abbess of Kildare and who died in 885. Her feast-day is 6 January. The name has been rendered *Talulla* and, in the seventeenth century, it was anglicised *Twilleliah*.

TAILLTIU: TAILLTE (tal'-t'e) f.   In Irish legend Tailltiu is nurse of Lug Lámfhota and she gave her name to Mag Tailten, where an important assembly of ancient Ireland was held. In other stories, she was daughter of the king of Spain and wife of Eochaid, the last king of the Fir Bolg who was slain in the battle of Mag Tuired. The name was rarely used in the later period. Tailltiu, daughter of Ua Máelechlainn king of Meath and wife of the great Turlough O Connor king of Ireland, died in 1127. This name has been latinised *Taltena*.

TAIRDELBACH: TOIRDHEALBHACH,   TRAOLACH, TÁRLACH (trē-lach, tār-lach) m, 'instigator, abettor'. Originally rare, this was a relatively popular name in the early period but it became extremely common in the later middle ages, possibly because it was borne by some of the greatest kings of the eleventh and twelfth centuries. Among its best-known bearers are Tairdelbach ua Briain, king of Munster and claimant to the kingship of Ireland, who died in 1086 and Tairdelbach ua Conchobair (Turlough O Connor), king of Connacht and king of Ireland, who died in 1156. In the later middle ages, it was a favourite name among the O Connors, O Briens, O Donnells, O Boyles, Mac Sweeneys and many other Irish families. In Donegal, where it was popular among the O Breslins, Mac Gillespies, Mac Sweeneys and O Gallaghers down to the nineteenth century, it was anglicised *Charles*. In the rest of Ireland and especially among the O Briens it became *Terence* and *Terry*. Among the modern dialectal variants are *Tárnaigh*, which was found in Omeath, *Tárlach*, *Tarla* and *Traolach*. The best anglicised form is *Turlough*.

TAITHLECH: TAICHLEACH (ta-l'ach) m, 'pacifying, placating'.   This name was much favoured throughout the medieval period by the O Dowds, O Haras, Mac Dermotts, and O Mulrooneys. From this name derives the rare surname Ó Taithligh (O Tally).

TANAIDE: TANAIDHE, TANAÍ (ton-ī) m, 'slender, subtle'. Tanaide Ua hUidir, abbot of Bangor, died in 958. In the later middle ages, this name was practically confined to the learned family of Ó Maolchonaire (O Mulconry, Conry).

TASSACH (tos-ach), m. Meaning, perhaps, 'idle, inactive'. In the legends of the saints Tassach was St Patrick's artisan. He was a bishop who gave St Patrick the last rites and his feast-day is 14 April.

TECHÁN: TEACHÁN (t'ach-ān) m, 'fair'. A rare early name.

TÉITE: TÉIDE (t'ē-d'e) f. Meaning, perhaps, 'wantonness'. In Irish legend Téite is daughter of Maicnia mac Lugdach and wife of Finn.

TEMAIR: TEAMHAIR (t'owr') f. Meaning, perhaps, 'eminence'. In Irish mythology Temair is the lady after whom the hill of Tara (*Temair*) is named. Temair was the name of the wife of the high-king Diarmait Rúanaid who died in 665. There is also a St Temair. This name could be anglicised *Tara*.

TEMNÉN: TEIMHNÍN (t'ev'-n'ín', t'ein'-ín') m. From *temen* 'dark'. There are two saints of the name, one whose feast-day is 7 August and another whose feast-day is 17 August. It has been suggested that the modern surname Tynan derives from this name.

TETHBA: TEATHBHA, TEAFA (t'af-a) f. In reality, Tethba is the early name of a district in Co Longford but in Irish legend, Tethba is daughter of the mythical king Eochu Airem. This name has been anglicised *Teffia*.

TIGERNACH: TIGHEARNACH, TIARNACH (t'īar-nach) m. From *tigern* 'a lord'. Among the saints who bore this name are St Tigernach, the bishop, whose feast-day is 17 March; St Tigernach of Clones whose feast-day is 4 April; and St Tigernach of Clonmacnoise and Roscommon who died in 1088. From this name derives the modern surname Ó Tighearnaigh (O Tierney).

TIGERNÁN: TIGHEARNÁN, TIARNÁN (t'īar-nān) m. From *tigern* 'lord, superior, chief'. An acceptable pet-form would be *Tiarn*, a modernisation of Old Irish *tigern*.

There was a St Tigernán of the shores of Lough Conn in Co Mayo whose feast-day is 8 April. There was a Tigernán of Uí Flaind (O Flynns) of Dál Cais, who were unsuccessful contenders for the kingship against the line of Brian in the tenth century. The name also occurs among the very early pedigrees of the Uí Aimbrit of Ciarraige Luachra. However, the name is inextricably linked with the royal race of the Uí Briúin of Breifne (Cavan, Leitrim and part of Longford) and was greatly favoured by the Uí Ruairc (O Rourkes), Meic Samradáin (Mac Govern) and Meic Thigernáin (Mac Kiernan). It remained in use among the O Rourkes down to the beginning of the modern period. Its most famous bearer was undoubtedly Tigernán Ua Ruairc, king of Breifne from about 1127 until 1172 when he was assassinated by the Anglo-Normans.

TIPRAITE: TIOBRAIDE (t'ub-rid'-e) m. This was a relatively common name in the early period. Tipraite mac Taidc, who died in 786, was king of Connacht as was Tipraite mac Dúnchada, who died in 718. Among its clerical bearers were Tipraite mac Ceithernaig, abbot of Clonfert, who died in 817 and Tipraite, abbot of Clonmacnoise, who died in 931. From this name derives the modern surname Ó Tiobraide (O Tubridy, Tubrit).

TÍRECHÁN: TÍREACHÁN (t'ir'-ach-ān) m, 'one possessed of lands, wide-ruling'. The best-known bearer of this name is bishop Tírechán, the biographer of St Patrick.

TÓLA (tō-la) m. Meaning, perhaps, 'abundance, flood'. The best-known bearer of this name is St Tóla of Dysart O Dea whose feast-day is 30 March.

TOMALTACH (tum-alt-ach) m. This name was particularly favoured by the Connachtmen in the middle ages and was common in the families of Mac Branan, Mac Donagh, Geraghty, O Beirne, O Mulrooney and Mac Dermott. It became obsolete in Ulster during the nineteenth century. It was anglicised *Thomas* (among the O Connors) and *Timothy*. From it derives the modern surname Tumelty.

*TOMÁS m. This is a borrowing of the biblical *Thomas*,

171

an Aramaic word meaning 'twin'. In Ireland, as in Anglo-Saxon England, this name was confined to clerics in the early middle ages. Among the early bearers of the name are Tomás, abbot and scribe of Bangor, who died in 794 and Tomás, bishop and scribe of Linn Duachaill, who died in 808. It was re-introduced by the Anglo-Normans, among whom it was a popular name, perhaps out of devotion to St Thomas a Beckett. The diminutive forms, *Tomag* and *Toimicín* occur in the fourteenth century. *Toimilin* which occurs among the Barretts of Connacht and the O Dohertys of Inishowen from the fourteenth century, may derive from this name.

TÓMMA: TUAMA (tūam-a) m. A rare early name borne by a saintly abbot of Bangor whose feast-day is 22 April. This name may be identical with the equally rare *Tuaim*, borne by an early king of Ossory. It is possible that this name is related to the modern surname Ó Tuama (O Twomey, Toomey).

TÓMMÁN (tōm-án) m, a diminutive form of *Tómma* (which see). This name was borne by the saintly bishop Tómmán whose feast-day is 18 March and by St Tómmán of Mungret whose feast-day is 26 July. There is a variant form of the name, *Tómméne*, *Tómmíne*, *Tuaimmíne* which was borne by St Tomméne of Lough Ooney, Co Monaghan, whose feast-day is 12 June and a saintly abbot of Armagh whose feast-day is 10 January.

TÓMNAT: TUAMNAIT (tūam-nit') f, a feminine form of *Tómmán* (which see).

TORCCÁN: TORCÁN (turk-án) m. From *torcc* 'wild boar'. A rare early name which occurs among the Eóganacht and the Dál Cais.

TORNA (tōr-na) m. Meaning, perhaps, 'puffed up'. Torna Éces was a legendary scholar of the ancient Irish. Perhaps for this reason it was greatly favoured by the learned family of Ó Maolchonaire (O Mulconry, Conry).

TRESSACH: TREASACH (tr'as-ach) m, 'warlike, fierce'. This name occurs occasionally in the early period. Among its bearers is Tressach mac Máel Muine, a petty king of the Limerick area, who died in 969. From this name is derived the modern surname Ó Treasaigh (O Tracey, Treacy).

TUATHAL (tūa-hal) m, 'ruler of the people'. This is the name of many Irish kings and heroes. Tuathal Techtmar was a legendary king and leader of the Goidelic invaders of Ireland according to some scholars. Tuathal Máelgarb was a sixth-century king of the Uí Néill. Tuathal mac Augaine (†958) was king of Leinster. In the later middle ages, this name was favoured by the bardic family Ó hUiginn (O Higgins), by the O Clerys and by the O Gallaghers. The name became obsolete in eastern Ulster in the middle of the nineteenth century but it survived in Donegal until the beginning of this century. It was generally anglicised *Toal* and *Tully*.

TUATHFLAITH: TUATHLAITH, TUATHLA (tūa-la) f. Meaning, originally, 'princess of the people'. This rare but beautiful name was borne by a queen of Leinster who died in 754.

u

UAINE (ūan'-e) f. This word means 'green, verdant', but Stokes felt that in this case it was an old word for 'a lady, a queen'. In the Finn-tales, Uaine Buide from Síd Duirnn Buide near Tonn Clídna is accompanied by all the birds from the Land of Promise and is the maker of the most wonderful music.

UAITHNE (ūa-n'e) m and f. This may be derived from *uainide* 'greenish' but in the later middle ages it is probably the tribal name Uaithne used as a personal name. There was an Uaithne (or Uainide) mac Donnubáin (†982) who was a petty king in the Limerick area. Conall Cearnach, the Ulster warrior, had a son called Uaithne and the same name was borne by the daughter of the legendary Munster king Eochaid mac Luchta. In the later middle ages, Uaithne was in use among the families of O Rourke, Mac Loughlin, O Reilly, O Hanley, Mageoghagan, O More and, at the very end of the middle ages, O Callaghan. It was anglicised *Oney, Oynie, Owney, Hewney*, on occasion *Anthony* and—by 'translation' from *Uaithne—Greene* among the O Molloys.

ULLACH (ūal-ach), f, 'proud, arrogant'. Uallach, daughter of Muimnechán, was chief poetess of Ireland and died in 934.

UALLACHÁN (ūal-ach-ān) m. From *uallach* 'proud'. From this name derives the modern surname Ó hUallacháin (O Hoolahan, Houghlahan, Houlihan).

UALLGARG (ūal-garg) m. From *uall* 'pride' and *garg* 'fierce'. This early name was greatly favoured by the O Rourkes and the Mac Kiernans in the middle ages. From it derives the surname Mac Uallgairg (Mac Goldrick).

UANFHIND: UAINIONN (ūan'-in) f, 'foam-white (of complexion)'. In the legends of the saints, Uanfhind is mother of St Mo Bí of Glasnevin.

UASAL (ūas-al) f, 'noble'. The name of an early female saint.

*UATÉR: UAITÉAR m. This is a borrowing of the Old German *Waldhar*, from *vald* 'rule' and *harja* folk'. It was brought to England by the Normans and brought thence to Ireland. The Irish forms reflect the medieval English forms *Wauter* and *Water* but the form *Ualtér* and the diminutives, *Uatín* and *Batín*, also occur in medieval Ireland.

*ÚGA m. This is the Germanic name, *Hugo* or *Hugh*, which was brought into Ireland by the Anglo-Normans. There is a diminutive form *Hughacc*. It has no connection with the Irish name *Áed*, which has almost invariably been translated *Hugh* in the post-medieval period.

*UILLECC: UILLEAG m. This is a diminutive of the borrowed name *Uilliam* (which see). It has been a favourite name among the Burkes of Connacht and a number of other families throughout the ages. It has been anglicised *Ulick* and, on occasion, *Ulysses*. *Uilleac* has been substituted for the Anglo-Norman borrowing, *Elias*, especially among the Walls and Mac Elligots.

*UILLIAM m. This is a borrowing of the Old German name *Willahelm*. The Normans brought it to England with the Conquest and thence introduced it to Ireland. It was common among the Burkes and other Anglo-Norman families. Among the Irish, it was especially favoured by the O Kellys. The diminutive form *Uillec* (which see) had made its appearance by the early fourteenth century. *Liam* is the current form in Irish.

ULTÁN (ul-tān) m, 'an Ulsterman'. Ultán is a relatively common name in the early period especially as the name of saints. Among the saints of the name are St Ultán, brother of St Fursu, whose feast-day is 27 April; St Ultán of Clooncorr, Co Roscommon, whose feast-day is 17 January; and, the best-known of all, St Ultán bishop of Arbracken and patron of children, whose feast-day is 4 September.

ÚNA (ūn-a) f.   This is an extremely popular name especially in later medieval Ireland. In legend, Úna Ollchrothach is daughter of the king of Lochlainn and mother of Conn Cétchathach. In later story, Úna Mac Dermott is the tragic lover of Tomás Láidir Costello and is the subject of the song *Úna Bhán*. In the nineteenth century, this name was anglicised *Winifred*, *Winny*, *Agnes* and *Unity*. It is now occasionally rendered *Oonagh*.

Index of variant forms

Abaigh	Abaigeal, Gobnat	*Animosus*	Anmchaid
		Anlon	Anlón
Abbey	Gobnat	*Anna*	Áine
Abbie	Gobnat	*Annalivia*	Life
Abigail	Gobnat	*Anne*	Áine, Eithne
Abina	Gobnat	*Annie*	Eithne
Aeneas	Éicnechán, Óengus	*Annora*	Onóra
		Anrahan	Ánrothán
Agnes	Mór, Úna	*Anthony*	Uaithne
Aherne	Echtigern	*Anvirre*	Ainmere
Ahiarn	Echtigern	*Aonghus*	Óengus
Aibhilín	Eibhlín	*Arabella*	Sibéal
Aidan	Áedán, Máedóc	*Archibald*	Gilla Epscoip
Aileen	Eibhlín	*Arnold*	Artgal
Albert	Ailbe, Beirichtir	*Arthur*	Art, Eochaid
		Artigan	Artucán
Alexander	Alusdar	*Ataigh*	Eochaid
Alice	Aislinn, Alis	*Atty*	Aithche
Alicia	Alis	*Augholy*	Echmhílidh
Alma	Almu	*Auley*	Amalgaid
Aloysius	Lugaid	*Auliffe*	Amlaíb
Alphonsus	Anlón	*Aurile*	Aurthuil
Alva	Álmath	*Avelina*	Eibhlín
Alva	Almu	*Averkagh*	Echmarcach
Amabel	Annábla	*Avnat*	Emnat
Ambrose	Anmchaid	*Awley*	Amalgaid
Anabel	Sibéal		
Angus	Óengus		

177

Bairre	Finbarr,	*Bidelia*	Brigit
	Barrfind	*Bidina*	Brigit
Barbara	Gormlaith	*Blanche*	Blinne
Barbary	Gormlaith	*Boethius*	Báethgalach,
Barclay	Parthalán		Buadach
Bardan	Barddán	*Bowes*	Báerhgalach
Barhan	Berchán	*Boyle*	Baígell
Barkley	Parthalán	*Brassal*	Bressal
Barnaby	Brian	*Breeda*	Brigit
Barney	Brian	*Breetha*	Brigit
Barra	Barrfind,	*Brenndán*	Brénainn
	Finnbar	*Brenda*	Brénainn
Barre	Barrfind,	*Brendan*	Brénainn
	Finnbarr	*Breslan*	Bresleán
Barry	Bairre,	*Briartach*	Muirchertach
	Barrfind,	*Bride*	Brigit
	Berach,	*Bridie*	Brigit
	Finnbarr	*Brídín*	Brigit
Bartley	Parthalán	*Brighdín*	Brigit
Basil	Bressal	*Brine*	Brian
Baskin	Baiscend	*Brissal*	Bressal
Batt	Parthalán	*Brochadh*	Murchad
Bazil	Brassal	*Brondus*	Donn
Beartlaoi	Parthalán	*Bryde*	Brigit
Beesy	Brigit		
Behellagh	Báethgalach		
Bella	Sibéal	*Caffar*	Cathbarr
Ben	Beirichtir	*Cahir*	Cathaír
Benignus	Benén	*Cain*	Cian
Benjamin	Beirichtir	*Cáit*	Caiterína
Bergin	Beirgíne	*Caitilín*	Caiterína
Berkely	Parthalán	*Cáitín*	Caiterína
Bernard	Beirichtir	*Caitríona*	Caiterína
Bertie	Ailbe,	*Callaghan*	Cellachán
	Beirichtir,	*Calvagh*	Calbhach
	Parthalán	*Canice*	Cainnech
Bessie	Sibéal	*Canoc*	Conmacc
Bid	Brigit	*Carina*	Cairenn
Biddle	Brigit	*Carthage*	Carthach
Biddy	Brigit	*Catholicus*	Cadlae,

	Cú Ulad	*Cosnaidhe*	Cosnumach
Cecily	Sibán	*Cowan*	Comgán
Celia	Síle	*Cowley*	Coblaith
Celsus	Cellach	*Cowvarre*	Cú Mara
Charles	Calbhach,	*Crehan*	Crimthann
	Cathaír,	*Cremin*	Cruimmíne
	Cathal, Cerball,	*Creon*	Crimthann
	Cormac,	*Criffin*	Crimthann
	Somhairle,	*Croney*	Crónán
	Tairdelbach	*Cud*	Conchobar
Christian	Gilla Críst	*Cullo*	Cú Ulad
Cinnéide	Cennétig	*Cullowe*	Cú Ulad
Clóideach	Clodagh	*Cumin*	Cuimmíne
Clora	Clothru	*Cummian*	Cuimmíne
Cohalan	Cathalán	*Curney*	Conchobar
Cohern	Cathchern	*Cuvea*	Cú Meda
Coilín	Nioclás	*Cyril*	Cairell
Colin	Cuilén		
Coll	Colla		
Colma	Colmán		
Comyn	Cuimmíne	*Dáibhí*	Dauíd
Con	Conchobar	*Daisey*	Onóra
Conle	Connla	*Dana*	Anu
Conleth	Conláed	*Daniel*	Domnall
Conley	Conláed	*Darby*	Diarmait
Conly	Connla	*Daroma*	Der Óma
Connell	Congal, Conall	*Davan*	Damán
Connor	Conchobar		Daimíne
Conny	Conchobar	*Davnit*	Damnat
Conry	Conrí	*Deasún*	Desmumhnach
Constance	Constans	*Debora(h)*	Gobnat
	Cosnumach	*Dora*	Gobnat
Constantine	Conn,	*Deegan*	Dubcenn
	Cosnumach,	*Delia*	Brigit
	Cú Chonnacht,	*Deman*	Demnán
	Causantín	*Denis*	Donnchad
Cooey	Cú Maige	*Derinn*	Der Finn
Cooley	Cú Ulad	*Dermot*	Diarmait
Cornelius	Conchobar	*Derry*	Diarmait
Corney	Conchobar	*Derval*	Derbáil

Dervila	Derbiled,		Dúnlang
	Der Bile	*Duggan*	Dubacán
Dervilia	Derbáil	*Dunan*	Dúnán
Dervin	Der Finn	*Duncan*	Donnchad,
Dervla	Der Bile		Dúnchán
Dervorgilla	Der bForgaill	*Dunla*	Dúnlaith
Desiderius	Accobrán	*Durkan*	Duarcán
Desmond	Desmumhnach	*Dymp(h)na*	Damnat
Devasse	Dub Essa		
Devnet	Damnat		
Didley	Dubaltach	*Éamonn*	Émann
Dillie	Brigit	*Eavan*	Aíbinn
Dina	Brigit	*Eavnat*	Aíbnat
Dinis	Donnchad	*Edan*	Áedán
Dionysius	Donnchad	*Eenis*	Óengus
Dolly	Doirend	*Egan*	Áeducán
Dolty	Dubaltach	*Eileen*	Eibhlín
Donagh	Donnchad	*Eily*	Eibhlín
Donaghy	Donnchad	*Ehir*	Aicher
Donald	Domnall	*Eleanor*	Ailionóra
Donat (us)	Donnchad	*Elias*	Ailill
Donegan	Donnucán		Uilleac
Donie	Domnall	*Eliza(beth)*	Sibéal
Dougal	Dubgall	*Ella*	Eibhlín
Donough	Donnchad	*Ellen*	Eibhlín
Donovan	Donndubán	*Ellie*	Eibhlín
Doogan	Dubacán	*Elsha*	Aislinn
Dorcan	Duarcán	*Ena*	Áednat,
Dorothy	Doirend		Eithne
Dorren	Doirend	*Enan*	Énán
Dorrie	Ferdorcha	*Enat*	Áedmat,
Dowd	Dubdae		Idnat
Dowling	Dúnlang	*Enda*	Énnae
Downet	Damnat	*Eneas*	Éicnechán,
Duald	Dubaltach		Óengus
Dualtagh	Dubaltach	*Enid*	Idnat
Dubhlang	Dúnlang	*Enos*	Óengus
Dudley	Dub dá leithe,	*Énrí*	Anraoi
	Dubgall,	*Eny*	Áednat
	Dubaltach,	*Erevan*	Éremón

180

Ernest	Ernán	Ferdinand	Feradach,
Esther	Aislinn		Ferdorcha,
Eugene	Eógan		Fergus,
Eugenius	Echmhílidh		Ferganainm
Eunan	Adamnán	Fergusius	Feradach
Eva	Aífe	Festie	Fachtna,
Evan	Eógan,		Fechín
	Émíne	Festus	Fachtna,
Eveleen	Eibhlín		Fechín,
Evegren	Aíbgréne		Fiachu
Evelina	Eibhlín	Fiacha	Fiachu
Evelyn	Eibhlín	Fidelma	Fedelm
Eveny	Aibne	Filorcia	Finnguala
Evin	Émíne	Finian	Finnén
Evle	Ébliu	Fin(n)bar(r)	Finnbarr
Evlin	Ébliu	Finnian	Finnén
Evnat	Emnat	Finnva	Finnmaith
Ewen	Eógan	Finola	Finnguala
		Fíona	Fíne
		Fiontan	Fintan
Fainder	Ainder	Flora	Finnguala
Fallon	Faithliu	Florence	Fíngin,
Fanahan	Finnchú		Fíthel,
Fanny	Fuinche		Flaithrí,
Fantasius	Fachtna		Flann
Farall	Fergal	Florrie	Fíngin
Farquhar	Ferchar	Florry	Fíngin,
Farrell	Fergal		Fíthel
Farry	Feradach	Flur	Fíngin
Farvila	Forbflaith	Francis	Proinnsias
Feagh	Fiachu	Frederick	Ferdorcha,
Feenat	Fiadnat		Feradach
Fehin	Fechín	Fursey	Fursu
Feidhlim	Fedelmid		
Felimy	Fedelmid		
Felix	Fedelmid		
Fenella	Finnguala	Garvan	Garbán
Fennet	Finnat	Garvin	Garbán
Fenmore	Finnabair	Gearóid	Geróit
Fenollina	Finnguala	Gelace	Gelgéid

Gelasius	Gillailsu, Glaisne	*Hercules*	Echdonn
Gene	Eógan	*Hewney*	Uaithne
Geoffrey	Goffraid, Séafraid	*Honor(a)*	Onóra
		Hugh(ie)	Áed, Cú Maige
Gertie	Gráinne	*Hugo*	Úga
Gertrude	Gráinne	*Humphrey*	Amlaíb
Gerald	Geróit		
Geraldine	Geróit	*Ida*	Íte
Geróitín	Geróit	*Ifor*	Ímar
Gilbert	Gilla Brigde	*Ignatius*	Éicnechán
Gilbrennan	Gilla Brénainn	*Irial*	Ailill
Gilbride	Gilla Brigde	*Irrill*	Ailill
Gilcole	Gilla Comgaill	*Irwin*	Éremón
Giles	Sibán	*Isabella*	Sibéal
Gilkevin	Gilla Cáemgein	*Ita*	Íte
Gilleece	Gilla Ísu	*Ivarr*	Ímar
Gilpatrick	Gilla Pátraic	*Ivor*	Ímar, Éber
Gobnet	Gobnat		
Gormley	Gormlaith		
Gorry	Goffraid		
Gotty	Goffraid	*Jacobus*	Sítae
Grace	Gráinne	*James*	Cú Ulad,
Granina	Gráinne		Glaisne,
Gregorius	Grimthann		Séamus
Greene	Uaithne	*Jarmy*	Diarmait
Griffin	Crimthann	*Jennie*	Síle
Grissel(da)	Gráinne	*Jeremiah*	Diarmait
Gubby	Gobnat	*Jeremy*	Diarmait
		Jerh	Diarmait
		Jerome	Cithruad, Diarmait
Haakon	Echdonn		
Hamish	Séamus	*Jerry*	Diarmait
Hannah	Áine, Onóra, Sibán	*Joan*	Sibán
		Johanna	Sibán
		John	Eógan, Eoin, Seaán
Hanorah	Onóra		
Harry	Anraoi, Éber	*Joseph*	Ioseph
Heber	Éber	*Judith*	Sibán, Sile,
Henry	Anraoi	*Judy*	Sibán, Síle

Julia	Síle, Sibán	*Lewis*	Laígsech,
Justin	Sáerbrethach		Lugaid
		Lewy	Lugaid
		Liam	Uilliam
Kálmán	Colmán	*Lizzie*	Sibéal
Kate	Caiterína	*Lochaigh*	Máel Sechnaill
Kathleen	Caiterína	*Loman*	Lommán
Katie	Caiterína	*Loran*	Luarán
Kathy	Caiterína	*Loughlin*	Lochlainn
Kay	Caiterína	*Louis*	Laígsech,
Kean(e)	Cian		Lugaid
Kedagh	Cétach	*Lucius*	Lachtna,
Kennedy	Cennétig		Laígsech
Kennelly	Cenn Fáelad	*Lucy*	Luigsech
Kenneth	Cináed	*Lynagh*	Laignech
Kenny	Cainnech	*Lysagh*	Laísech
Kerill	Cairell		
Kevin	Cáemgen		
Kiely	Cadlae	*Mab*	Medb
Kieran	Ciarán	*Mabbie*	Medb
Kihrooe	Cithruad	*Mabbina*	Medb
Kilian	Cilléne	*Mabel*	Annábla
King	Cian	*Mable*	Medb
Kinsella	Cennselach	*Macartan*	Mac Cáirthinn
Kit(ty)	Caiterína	*Macbeth*	Mac Bethad
Kyne	Cadan	*Maccon*	Mac Con
		Madge	Márgrég, Medb
			Muirenn
Lachlan	Lochlainn	*Máedóc*	Áedán
Laoiseach	Lachtna	*Maeve*	Medb
Laserian	Laisrén	*Mag(ey)*	Márgrég
Lasrina	Lassar Fhína	*Maggie*	Márgrég
Lassarina	Lassar Fhína	*Magonius*	Máenach
Laughlin	Lochlainn	*Mahon*	Mathgamain
Laurence	Lochlainn,	*Máille*	Máire
	Lorcán	*Mailse*	Máire
Lazarus	Mo Laisse,	*Mailti*	Máire
	Laisrén	*Máirín*	Máire
Leanan	Liadnán	*Máirtín*	Martan
Lennan	Lennán	*Maisie*	Márgrég

Maitiú	Maiú		Máel Mórda
Malachias	Máel Máedóc	*Milo*	Máel Muire
Malachy	Máel Máedóc,	*Mogue*	Máedóc, Áedá
	Máel Sechnaill	*Moira*	Máire
Malcolm	Máel Coluim	*Móirín*	Mór
Mallaidh	Máire	*Moll(y)*	Máire
Mamie	Máire	*Mona(t)*	Muadnat
Manasses	Magnus	*Monica*	Moncha
Mannix	Mainchíne	*Monty*	Muirchertach
Manus	Magnus	*Mór*	Máire
Margery	Máire	*Mór*	Móirne
Maria, -e	Máire	*Moreen*	Mór
Marianus	Máel Muire	*Morgan*	Murchad
Marion	Muirenn	*Moriartogh*	Muirchertach
Marjory	Máire	*Morina*	Mór
Martha	Mór	*Morrianus*	Máel Ruanaid
Martin	Martan	*Mortimer*	Muirchertach
Mary	Máire, Mór	*Moses*	Magnus,
Matha	Maiú		Máedóc
Matheus	Mathgamain	*Moyra*	Máire
Matthew	Maiú, Matha,	*Mreartach*	Muirchertach
	Mathgamain	*Mulroney*	Máel Ruanaid
Maud	Medb	*Multose*	Eiltín
Maura	Máire	*Munchin*	Mainchíne
Maureen	Máire	*Murianus*	Máel Ruanaid
Maurice	Muirchertach,	*Muriel*	Muirgel
	Muirgius	*Murray*	Máel Muire
Mauricius	Muirchertach	*Murrough*	Murchad
Maurus	Murchad	*Murry*	Muiredach
May	Máire	*Murt(y)*	Muirchertach
Mealmoe	Máel Muad	*Murtaugh*	Muirchertach
Méars	Máire	*Myles*	Máel Muire,
Meeda	Íte		Máel Ruanaid
Meg	Márgrég	*Myrun*	Muirenn
Meidhbhín	Medb		
Meyler	Máel Muire		
Miah	Diarmait	*Nábla*	Annábla
Míde	Íte	*Nahor*	Conchobar
Miles	Máel Muire,	*Nanno*	Onóra

184

Nappy	Finnguala	*Orna(t)*	Odornat
Naos	Óengus	*Ossian*	Oissíne
Narvla	Nárbflaith	*Owein*	Augaine
Nathy	Nath-í	*Owen*	Eógan
Naugher	Conchobar	*Owney*	Uaithne
Neas	Éicnechán	*Oyne*	Eógan, Uaithne
Neelusheen	Conchobar	*Oynie*	Eógan
Neese	Óengus		
Nehemias	Gilla na Náem	*Padhra*	Pátraic
Neil	Conchobar	*Padraigín*	Pátraic
Néill	Niall	*Páid(í)*	Pátraic
Nelius	Conchobar	*Páidín*	Pátraic
Niall	Nioclás	*Páraic*	Pátraic
Nicholas	Óengus, Niall,	*Parra*	Pátraic
	Coilín	*Partnán*	Parthalán
Niece	Óengus	*Patrick*	Pátraic,
Noah	Noíse		Gilla Pátraic
Nohor	Conchobar	*Peig(í)*	Márgrég
Nóinín	Onóra	*Penelope*	Finnguala
Nóirín	Onóra	*Penny*	Finnguala
Nonie	Onóra, Sibán	*Peregrine*	Cú Choigcríche
Nóra	Onóra	*Peter*	Máel Petair,
Norah	Onóra		Peadar, Piaras,
Noreen	Onóra		Feoras
Nuala	Finnguala	*Phelim*	Fedelmid
Nyce	Noíse	*Philip*	Fedelmid Pilib
		Philpog	Pilib
		Piarag	Piaras
Obscurus	Ferdorcha	*Piers*	Piaras, Feoras
Oghe	Eochaid	*Preanndaigh*	Proinnsias
Oghie	Eochaid		
Oho	Eochaid		
Olaf	Amlaíb	*Quinlan*	Caíndelbán
Olan	Eolang	*Quinlevan*	Caíndelbán
Oliver	Olibhéar,	*Quintin*	Cú Maige
	Ailill	*Quinton*	Cú Maige
Onan	Adamnán		
Oney	Uaithne		
Oonagh	Úna		
Oran	Odrán	*Randal*	Ragnall

185

Rannal	Ragnall	*Sheila*	Síle
Rearden	Rígbarddán	*Shelagh*	Síle
Redmond	Rémann	*Shiela*	Síle
Regina	Rígnach,	*Siacas*	Séamus
	Ragnailt	*Sibby*	Sibéal
Rhoddy	Ruaidrí	*Sidney*	Sétna
Richard	Ruaidrí,	*Siomataigh*	Séamus
	Ricard	*Simon*	Senán, Suibne
Ríona	Caiterína	*Sinan*	Senán
Riordan	Rígbarddán	*Sinéad*	Sibán
Risdeag	Ricard	*Sinon*	Senán
Risderd	Ricard	*Siomaigh*	Séamus
Roddy	Ruaidrí	*Sive*	Sadb
Roderick	Ruaidrí	*Slanina*	Sláine
Róisín	Róis	*Sleimhne*	Stiamna
Rosa	Ross	*Solomon*	Solamn
Rowan	Rúadán	*Sophia*	Sadb
		Sophy	Sadb
		Sorley	Somhairle
Sabia	Sadb	*Standish*	Ainéislis
Sabina	Sadb, Síle	*Stanislaus*	Ainéislis
Saibhne	Suibne	*Stephen*	Stiamna
Sally	Sadb, Síle,	*Stiofán*	Stiamna
	Sorcha	*Susan(na)*	Sibán
Samuel	Somhairle	*Sybil*	Sibéal
Sarah	Sadb, Sorcha	*Synan*	Senán
Seán	Eoin, Seaán		
Séartha	Séafraid		
Seathrún	Séafraid	*Taltena*	Tailitiu
Seeva	Síthmaith	*Talulla*	Tailefhlaith
Selia	Síle	*Tara*	Temair
Senan	Senán	*Tarla*	Tairdelbach
Seóan	Seaán	*Tárlach*	Tairdelbach
Seóinín	Seaán	*Tárnaigh*	Tairdelbach
Seón	Seaán, Eoin	*Teague*	Tadc
Seosamh	Ioseph	*Ted*	Tadc
Shane '	Seaán	*Teffia*	Tethba
Shay	Ségdae	*Terence*	Tairdelbach
Sheedy	Sítae	*Terry*	Tairdelbach
Sheela	Síle	*Thaddeus*	Tadc